SpringerBriefs in Criminology

International and Comparative Criminology

Series Editor
Ernesto U. Savona, Transcrime, Università Cattolica del Sacro Cuore di Milano, Milan, Italy

More information about this series at http://www.springer.com/series/11921

Alberto Aziani

Illicit Financial Flows

An Innovative Approach to Estimation

Springer

Alberto Aziani
Transcrime
Università Cattolica del Sacro Cuore
Milano, Italy

ISSN 2192-8533 ISSN 2192-8541 (electronic)
SpringerBriefs in Criminology
ISSN 2365-841X ISSN 2365-8428 (electronic)
International and Comparative Criminology
ISBN 978-3-030-01889-4 ISBN 978-3-030-01890-0 (eBook)
https://doi.org/10.1007/978-3-030-01890-0

Library of Congress Control Number: 2018958478

This Springer imprint is published by the registered company Springer Nature Switzerland AG
The registered company address is: Gewerbestrasse 11, 6330 Cham, Switzerland

Acknowledgments

I would like to sincerely thank my colleagues and friends whose insightful points of view, comments, and assistance helped me in producing this book, especially Giulia Berlusconi, Francesco Calderoni, Serena Favarin, Luca Giommoni, Martina Marchesi, Pietro Minotti, Michele Riccardi, Federico Sallusti, and Ernesto U. Savona.

I am very grateful to the Research and Trend Analysis Branch of the UNODC, specifically Enrico Bisogno, Diana Camerini, Alexander Kamprad, Angela Me, and Irmgard Zeiler who provided me with the opportunity to join the UNODC-UNCTAD Expert consultation on the SDG Indicator on illicit financial flows, held in Vienna in December 2017. Participating with them in these workshops and discussions proved to be inspiring and fruitful in terms of the development of this book.

Finally, I would like to thank Ilaria Mastro for her support with the graphical layout.

Introduction

The term "illicit financial flows" (IFFs) has come to prominence in recent decades. The hype around IFFs is reflective of significant shifts within the international criminological landscape. Firstly, there was a series of scandals involving autocrats misappropriating fortunes and impoverishing the countries over which they rule; secondly, there is a growing concern about the ramifications of an insufficiently regulated, and apparently increasingly predatory, international financial system; thirdly, there is an emergent trust in follow-the-money policies to defeat "global bads," namely, corruption, organized crime, transnational crimes, and terrorism.

Significant outflows of capital from developing countries reduce domestic resource mobilization and slow down sustainable economic growth (Clark 2011; Kar and Spanjers 2015); indeed, the consequences of this have been so severe that, today, acknowledging that IFFs can have detrimental effects on economic growth and poverty alleviation has become a mainstream position in development economics (Herkenrath 2014; Reuter 2012). The depression of the fiscal policies is not the only reason that the spotlight has been shone on IFFs. In conjunction with economic and political elites, civil society has a key role to play in terms of defending and cultivating the rule of law. Hence, leaders who move vast fortunes abroad and plunder their country can undermine trust in public institutions and, in turn, trigger a vicious cycle of negative behavior. At the same time, these very same elites are less incentivized to work toward advancing their local economic system, defend property rights and the efficiency of civil trials, when their capital is safely stored abroad (Reuter 2017).

Despite its centrality in debates about developing countries, the harm caused by IFFs is not specific to these countries. With respect to advanced economies, the 2008 global financial crisis brought the topic into acute focus. The propagation of the crisis brutally underlined the incapacity of national regulatory tools to counter and address the financial operations of private actors operating in a global environment (Blankenburg and Khan 2012). Today, discussion around the introduction of turnover taxes for the elusive big tech firms, such as Google, Facebook, and Amazon, underscores further the necessity to deal with IFFs at a global level. Indeed, according to the European Commission (2018), by re-routing some of their profits to low-tax member states, the top digital firms face an effective tax rate of only 9.5%, less than half the level of traditional companies, which poses serious questions with respect to competition, tax revenue losses, and, more generally, fairness.

Finally, a third area of concern centers on how IFFs may impact on societies by facilitating the commission of serious crimes and allowing for the financing of terrorist movements (Blankenburg and Khan 2012; Levi 2010; Schneider 2008; UNODC 2017). Within this perspective, the focus on IFFs is not so much driven by a concern for the draining of public resources as it is by the threats posed by the predicate crimes of IFFs. Effectively countering IFFs is viewed as an instrument through which to tackle criminal activities, which offer high revenues to their participants. Given that economic profit is the principal driver of involvement in most crimes, impeding criminals' ability to enjoy the fruits of their labor would appear to be a reasonable strategy to fight crime. After all, who would risk severe punishment or even their life to acquire good money if they have no means through which to safely conceal, transfer, and spend the money?

The contemporary relevance of IFFs is such that reducing IFFs is now a staple of declarations from the G8 and G20, which urge countries to counter IFFs on several fronts. For instance, countries should strengthen their anti-money laundering regimes; enforce greater transparency over company ownership; support efforts to trace, freeze, and recover stolen assets; develop automatic exchanges of information systems; and tackle tax evasion (OECD 2014). However, the fight against IFFs is not only a priority for the major industrialized countries but also for other international institutions, such as the World Bank and especially the United Nations. On July 27, 2015, the General Assembly of the United Nations adopted the Addis Ababa Action Agenda which invites "appropriate international institutions and regional organizations to publish estimates of the volume and composition of illicit financial flows" (2015, p. 8). Moreover, by adopting this agenda, United Nations Member States are committing themselves to "redouble efforts to substantially reduce illicit financial flows by 2030, with a view to eventually eliminating them" (2015, p. 8).

The institutional attention granted to the measurement of IFFs as an important tool through which to engender economic development gained further prominence when the General Assembly of the United Nations adopted the global indicator framework on July 6, 2017. Within this framework, the United Nations stresses that the development of a methodology to estimate IFFs is necessary so as to comply with the data requirements stemming from the global Sustainable Development Goal (SDG) indicator framework (United Nations 2017). More specifically, the UN Statistical Commission has identified the indicator 16.4.1 "Total value of inward and outward IFFs (in current US dollars)" as the global metric to monitor 16.4 target of the SDGs (i.e., "By 2030, significantly reduce illicit financial and arms flows, strengthen the recovery and return of stolen assets and combat all forms of organized crime"), allied with the indicator 16.4.2 on illicit firearms trafficking (i.e., "Proportion of seized and small arms and light weapons that are recorded and traced, in accordance with international standards and legal instruments").

The aforementioned institutional enthusiasm is dampened by the fact that the development of a sound methodology through which to estimate IFFs is plagued by several issues. Although the term itself is generally used to designate the international transfer of money, which is related to illicit activities in its generation, transfer or use phases, there is hitherto no universal agreement on this classification, and, indeed, different stakeholders understand it in wholly distinct ways. Moreover, such a definition is undoubtedly broad and encompasses a suite of behavior and actions; IFF can thus be understood as an umbrella term for a broad group of cross-border economic and financial transactions, ranging from very simple tax abuse schemes to extremely complex money laundering operations. Therefore, the first set of issues pertains to the difficulty in developing a universally adopted definition of the phenomenon and operationalizing it. A second set of issues refers to the statistical feasibility of quantifying IFFs, which, like most crime-related phenomena, is extremely challenging. This is because IFFs, and the underlying predicate offences, are purposefully hidden or disguised by criminals who, evidently, are seeking to protect themselves from the interventions of law enforcement agencies. Consequently, attempting to gather reliable information to model criminal actions and the requisite data through which to accurately measure their outcomes can be challenging to say the least.

This book addresses these as yet unresolved issues pertaining to the conceptualization and estimation of IFFs, rather than analyzing the consequences of the outflow of capital from developing countries, or focusing on how financial systems could mitigate the effects of IFFs. Over the course of the book, I propose a reorganization and schematization of theoretical and statistical doxa about IFFs. The hope is that the critical evaluation of the current definitions and estimation strategies will help the reader better understand the underlying principles of IFFs and the inherent difficulties involved in analyzing IFFs. Moving on from this analysis of the current state of the situation, the second part of the book lays forth a contribution to the estimate of IFFs introducing the *flow-network approach*. The book is structured in terms of an introduction, four main chapters, and conclusions.

Chapter 1 concentrates on definitional and conceptual issues. To this day, there is a notable ambiguity in definitions of IFFs. The main issues center on the use of the word illicit. The meaning of illicit is broader than the term illegal and, according to certain strands of thought, encompasses a host of ambiguous transfer practices that are aimed at reducing taxation. More generally, the phenomena that are included within the boundaries of definitions of IFFs are so numerous and diverse as to raise questions about both its ability as an explanatory concept and its expedience for designing effective policies.

Chapter 2 describes the main approaches for estimating IFFs in extant literature and considers the underlying ideas and the data required for analysis, along with outlining the manifold limitations of the respective methods. The semantic and conceptual difficulties involved in interpreting IFFs, allied with the broadness of the definition itself, are echoed in its operationalization and the design of the methods used to estimate it. Overall, all the proposed methods suffer from several limitations, some of which appear to be insurmountable. The development of any reliable synthetic indicator of IFFs thus requires breaking IFFs down into its constituent components, allied with a strong internal sense of consistency, which would ultimately improve the accuracy of the estimates.

Chapter 3 outlines an innovative method for estimating IFFs, informed by the review of conceptual debates and critical evaluation of extant estimation methods in the earlier chapters. In contradistinction to other currently available methods, the proposed *flow-network approach* permits to estimate inward and outward IFFs related to the transnational trafficking of illicit goods. This strategy also allows for the overall estimation of the gross value added related to transnational trafficking, from whence it becomes potentially possible to estimate money laundering-related IFFs, once the requisite information becomes available. Of course, the resulting estimate is not without its limitations, but, nevertheless, it permits the linking of IFFs to their predicate offences, overcomes double counting issues, and permits cross-national and longitudinal comparisons. Moreover, it is a unique instrument through which to better understand and contrast the predicate crimes of IFFs. Finally, it increases our understanding of illicit industries by giving us an insight into their economic scope. While I specifically utilize the trafficking of cocaine as an illustrative example, the same approach can be applied to any other form of trafficking, as far as the requisite data is available.

Chapter 4 provides a critical exploration of the limitations of the proposed *flow-network approach*, its underlying data, and the assumptions that are involved in its usage. At the same time, it examines at length the calculi required to perform the analysis through recourse to examples and reasoning about the proceeds generated from cocaine trafficking. The step-by-step description of the entire methodology is driven by the fact that the illegality of trafficking activities makes it difficult to estimate their overall size and value, a point which forces one to adopt numerous assumptions. The chapter concludes by arguing that only by carefully assessing the data, underlying assumptions, and limitations of the adopted method can researchers correctly interpret the results and continue to refine the methods.

References

Blankenburg, S., & Khan, M. (2012). Governance and illicit flows. In P. H. Reuter (Ed.), *Draining development? Controlling flows of illicit funds from developing countries* (pp. 21–68). Washington, DC: The World Bank http://documents.worldbank.org/curated/en/305601468178737192/Draining-development-Controlling-flows-of-illicit-funds-from-developing-countries

Clark, H. (2011). *Clark: Illicit finances divert resources away from development*. United Nations Development Programme http://www.undp.org/content/undp/en/home/presscenter/speeches/2011/05/11/clark-illicit-finances-divert-resources-away-from-development.html

European Commission. (2018). *Questions and answers on a fair and efficient tax system in the EU for the digital single market*. European Commission http://europa.eu/rapid/press-release_MEMO-18-2141_en.htm

Herkenrath, M. (2014). Illicit financial flows and their developmental impacts: An overview. *International Development Policy/Revue Internationale de Politique de Développement, 5*(5.3).

Kar, D., & Spanjers, J. (2015). Illicit financial flows from developing countries. In *Global financial integrity* (pp. 2004–2013). Washington, DC: http://www.gfintegrity.org/report/illicit-financial-flows-from-developing-countries-2004-2013/

Levi, M. (2010). Combating the financing of terrorism: A history and assessment of the control of 'threat finance'. *The British Journal of Criminology, 50*(4), 650–669.

OECD. (2014). *Illicit financial flows from developing countries: measuring OECD responses*. Paris: Organisation for Economic Co-operation and Development – OECD https://www.oecd.org/corruption/Illicit_Financial_Flows_from_Developing_Countries.pdf

Reuter, P. H. (2012). *Draining development? Controlling flows of illicit funds from developing countries*. 66815. The World Bank. http://documents.worldbank.org/curated/en/305601468178737192/Draining-development-Controlling-flows-of-illicit-funds-from-developing-countries

Reuter, P. H. (2017). *Illicit financial flows and governance: The importance of disaggregation*. World Bank http://pubdocs.worldbank.org/en/677011485539750208/WDR17-BP-Illicit-Financial-Flows.pdf

Schneider, F. (2008). Money laundering and financial means of organised crime: Some preliminary empirical findings. *Global Business and Economics Review, 10*(3), 309–330.

United Nations. (2017). Home — SDG indicators. *Sustainable Development Goal Indicators Website, 2017* https://unstats.un.org/sdgs/

United Nations General Assembly. (2015). *Resolution adopted by the general assembly on 27 July 2015*. http://www.un.org/ga/search/view_doc.asp?symbol=A/RES/69/313

UNODC. (2017). *World drug report 2017*. Vienna: United Nations Office on Drugs and Crime https://www.unodc.org/wdr2017/index.html

Contents

List of Figures

List of Tables

About the Author

Alberto Aziani is a research fellow at Università Cattolica del Sacro Cuore in Milan and senior researcher at Transcrime. He holds an MSc in Economics and Social Sciences and a PhD in Criminology. His research interests are transnational and organized crime. He has conducted studies on these topics and collaborated with the UNODC and the EC on research projects examining drug trafficking and money laundering in relation to illicit markets.

Chapter 1
Illicit Financial Flows: Conceptual and Operational Issues

1.1 Introduction

The concept of illicit financial flows (IFFs) is undeniably complex. Indeed, the term encompasses a range of activities including hiding the proceeds of trafficking, theft, corruption, embezzlement, channeling funds into criminal enterprises and terrorism financing, profit shifting in order to evade or elude taxes, and capital flight in non-compliance with currency controls and other regulations for cross-border transactions. Criminals exploit multiple channels and methods in order to perform each of these activities. Consequently, while the definition of IFFs as cross-border movements of money and other assets associated with illicit activities is accepted by most scholars and institutions, there is still ambiguity with respect to the actual interpretation and understanding of IFFs.

Hence, a deeper examination of the concept of IFFs is necessary at this juncture, especially given that the term is gaining increased *momentum*; specifically, several questions must be answered pertaining to measuring and combating predicate offenses and designing effective development policies. Is IFF the most expedient concept through which to frame the problem? Should the concept exclusively address financial flows related to illegal actions, or should a broader conception be adopted that takes into account actions which are not manifestly against the law but nevertheless have detrimental societal effects? Given the available definitions, is any estimate of IFFs feasible or useful?

This chapter provides an overview of how IFFs are defined and conceptualized within extant literature and, ultimately, advocates for their clarification. The chapter is structured as follows. The opening section examines the most cited definitions of IFFs in an attempt to identify points of convergence and trace the limits of the proposed conceptualizations. The second section delineates a conceptual framework about the illegitimacy of the generation, transfer, and use of money so as to better comprehend what the definitions of IFF actually encompass. Subsequently, through

A. Aziani, *Illicit Financial Flows*, SpringerBriefs in Criminology,
https://doi.org/10.1007/978-3-030-01890-0_1

recourse to money laundering (ML) and tax evasion literature predominantly, the third section illustrates the principal methods through which money is moved illegitimately across countries. The final section reflects upon the key issues and challenges pertaining to defining and conceptualizing IFFs.

1.2 The Problematic Definition of a Fashionable Concept

The term illicit financial flows first emerged in the 1990s, where it was principally associated with the idea of capital flight, that is, the outflow of financial assets and capital from a nation due to political or economic instability, currency devaluation, the imposition of capital controls, or increased taxation (World Bank, 2017). Subsequently, many governments and international institutions have come to routinely use the term illicit financial flows; indeed, the term has become so accepted that it is now primarily referred to in its abbreviated form of IFFs. According to Baker (2015), the success of the term IFF derives, in part, from its superiority to alternative phrasings, such as *illegal capital flight*, *dirty money*, and others. Firstly, illicit is a less stringent word than illegal, which means that economists, lawyers, and policymakers can use it in a more flexible manner. Secondly, the word financial underscores that the focus is on money as opposed to trafficking or flows of illicit goods. Thirdly, as Baker observes, "flows is perhaps the most important word, making it clear that what is being addressed has an origin and a path and a destination" (2015, 1). However, in reality, not all stakeholders currently agree on the exact meaning of the terms illicit, financial, and flow, and, as such, agreeing upon a suitable definition of IFF remains a contentious issue (Reuter, 2017; World Bank, 2017). While the increasing popularity of the acronym IFF is beyond question, its actual meaningfulness and usefulness in terms of policymaking and measurement are debatable.

Despite the growing attention, IFFs hitherto are undefined in the international normative framework, and, indeed, different institutions and authors interpret it in manifold ways. Kar (2010, 1), the chief economist at Global Financial Integrity, a nonprofit organization and one of the main institutions advocating the use of the term IFFs, defines them as "money that is illegally earned, transferred, or utilized. Somewhere at its origin, movement, or use, the money broke laws and hence it is considered illicit." UNECA (2015, 23) advocates a similar definition: "money illegally earned, transferred or used," while the World Bank (2017, 1) proposes an almost identical definition of IFF but with emphasis on the transnational nature of the flow – "money illegally earned, transferred, or used that crosses borders." Clark (2011, 1), administrator of the UNDP, underlines the illegality of the earning phase and the cross-border dimension of IFF, purporting that "illicit flows include, but are not limited to, cross-border transfers of the proceeds of tax evasion, corruption, trade in contraband goods, and criminal activities such as drug trafficking and counterfeiting." The OECD (2014, 16) states "[t]here are various definitions of illicit financial flows, but essentially they are generated by methods, practices and crimes aiming to transfer financial capital out of a country in contravention of national or international laws." Similarly, according to the *Coherent policies for combatting Illicit Financial Flows* by the UNODC/OECD (2016, 3), "IFFs are defined broadly as all cross-border financial transfers, which contravene national or international laws." Finally, Epstein (2005, 7) defines IFFs as "capital taken abroad in a hidden form, perhaps because it is illegal, or perhaps because it goes against social norms, or perhaps because it might be vulnerable to economic or political threat." As one can discern from the above definitions, despite some key points of overlap, there nevertheless remain several challenges in designating what in fact IFFs refer to.

1.2.1 Illicit

There are two meanings for the word illicit in the English language. The Cambridge dictionary defines the term illicit as "illegal or disapproved of by society," while the Oxford dictionary defines it as "forbidden by law, rules or custom." Consequently, it is perhaps unsurprising that there are also two predominant interpretations of the word illicit that characterize the work of those scholars aiming to operationalize the concept of IFFs: normative and law-based (Forstater, 2018; Reuter, 2017). The normative interpretation suggests that financial flows become illicit because they are deemed illegitimate from the perspective of an existing consensus about the social good. Thus, here illicit flows are defined in relation to socially and/or morally unacceptable, or simply undesirable, activities, rather than necessarily being in contravention of official laws (Blankenburg & Khan, 2012). In contrast, the law-based approach designates IFF as that which is contrary to or forbidden by law, especially criminal law (see Fig. 1.1).

Resultantly, the question as to whether it is more meaningful to reason in terms of illegality (i.e., law-based interpretation) or in terms of social disapproval (i.e., normative interpretation) is not a straightforward one. This distinction is especially important when attempting to measure IFFs, especially with respect to those ones that are connected to profit shifting as a means through which to reduce taxation. In relation to the above example, a purely legal interpretation would only focus on the illegal practices of tax evasion, whereas a more inclusive normative interpretation would view IFF in terms of the entire spectrum of possibilities of illegal evasion and legal avoidance (Cobham & Janský, 2017b; Picciotto, 2011). Hence, the adoption of a normative interpretation tends to lead to a higher estimate of IFFs. The important point to consider here is that, while many would consider profit shifting as an illicit action that subtracts funds from the countries where actual profits have been generated, others, such as the multinational companies actuating these practices, would not (Baker, 2005).

With respect to profit shifting, then the normative interpretation is more inclusive than the law-based perspective. However, adopting a normative approach might result in lower estimates of IFFs than if one embraced the law-based approach and focused on the proceeds of crime. Moreover, while ordinarily what is illegal is also

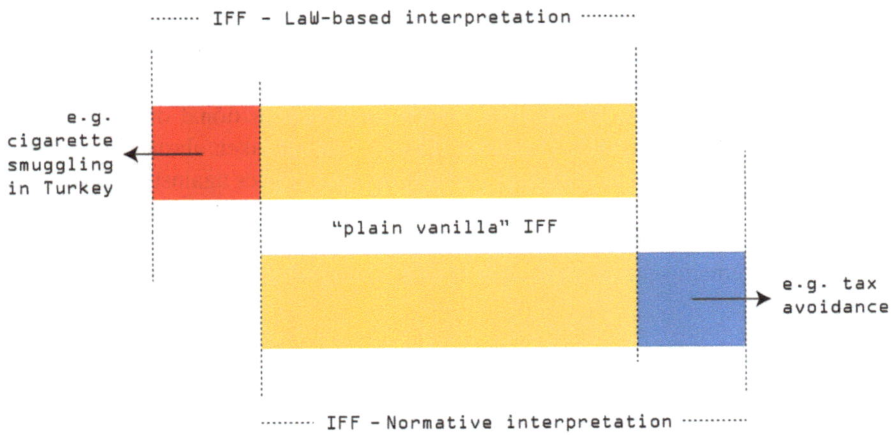

Fig. 1.1 Conceptual map of the differences and overlaps of the law-based and normative definitions of IFFs.
Note: Most IFFs can be understood through both law-based (i.e., financial flows are illicit because they are related to activities that are forbidden by the law) and normative interpretations (i.e., financial flows are illicit because they are related to activities that are against the social good), but this does not mean that the two concepts fully overlap. Indeed, there are activities which are not explicitly forbidden by any law but whose consequences might be detrimental for society (e.g., tax avoidance), whereas in specific contexts, albeit less frequently, practices like tax evasion or smuggling are socially accepted while being expressly forbidden by the law. (Source: author's elaboration)

illicit, this is not always the case. In southeastern Turkey, for example, smuggling cigarettes enjoys a certain degree of social acceptance, even though it is technically an illegal practice outlawed under national criminal law. Many inhabitants of the region justify smuggling because they consider the state to be responsible for their disadvantaged socioeconomic circumstances (Melzer, 2010). With respect to this example, authors operating within a normative perspective would not include in IFFs the movement of the proceeds stemming from cigarette smuggling. By contrast, drug trafficking is not socially accepted, but is widespread in the same area (Melzer, 2010) and, therefore, would be taken into account in estimates of IFFs by both law-based and normative approaches.

Moreover, legal principals themselves are often blurred in the sense that they depend on interpretations which, in turn, are influenced by the broader social context and their teleological nature (Picciotto, 2007); hence, in an international situation, it is not straightforward to define if a behavior is actually illegal or not. Indeed, countries may have different laws, and thus clarity would be needed about how to consider flows that are fully legal in one country, but illegal in another jurisdiction. Finally, if the express aim is to measure IFFs, then one must take into consideration cross-national disparities in detecting and registering crime. For example, tax authorities in a low-income country may lack the administrative instruments to discover and successfully challenge in court a hypothetical case of commercial tax evasion. In a country with more robust institutions, the same exact behavior would be more readily identified and brought in front of a court. Therefore, a strictly legal definition of IFF would lead to a systematic underestimation of IFFs in states with a less effective rule of law (Cobham & Janský, 2017a).

Alternatively, we could shift our analytical gaze onto the harm caused by an action, rather than, say, the question of legality and/or acceptance of the action itself (Dorling et al., 2008; Global Initiative, 2018). Adopting this perspective brings into sharp focus the noxious consequences of a given action. Hence, aggressive tax avoidance schemes would be included in the calculi of IFFs, because they drain important resources away from countries, which, in turn, disproportionately affects less affluent members of society. Overall, then, law-based, normative, and harm-centered interpretations all have their respective strengths and limitations with respect to depicting certain phenomena, allowing for cross-national comparability, and permitting certain measurements. The choice to adopt one perspective over another primarily depends on the purpose of the analysis, the crimes to be examined, the geopolitical scope of the analysis, data availability, and other factors. In light of these options, it is imperative to clearly state which approach one is taking, why it has been adopted, and how the results should be interpreted in relation to the choices that the researcher has made.

1.2.2 Financial

Although IFF ordinarily refers to flows of money (Reuter, 2017), the term "financial" can be understood as more than simply monetary flow; it can refer to physical products, intangible assets, opportunities, and gains. For example, drug traffickers are known to barter their loads for firearms, oil, or other products they may directly need or can easily resell. Scholars have also observed the use of bartering in the smuggling of oil, wildlife, and other forms of transnational trafficking (e.g., Barakat, 2008; Steinberg, 2005). The trade of intangible assets in exchange for promises of future advantages or political support has also been widely documented in relation to corruption practices and tax evasion schemes (Baker, 2005; OECD, 2000; Reuter, 2017). Patents and trademarks constitute other intangible assets that can be exploited to shift profits from country to country to minimize corporate profits (Dischinger & Riedel, 2011).

Whether or not to focus solely on money is an important initial choice when adopting certain IFF estimation strategies. Indeed, estimates produced with misalignment strategies are only capable of focusing on the monetary values of IFFs, because of the data they rely upon. In contrast, it is much more challenging to measure bartering practices or attempt to quantify the value of an asset which is intangible. Moreover, focusing solely on money simplifies the production of estimates that do not require the combination of different flows based on different unit of measures. The monetary value of the flow is also the easiest means through which to present estimates of IFFs and compare them with GDP or other economic indicators. Nonetheless, the exploitation of other kinds of assets in ML and trafficking practices could prove relevant for both specific crimes and regions and, consequently, should be addressed. Once again, the plurality of meaning with respect to the term financial itself does not help initiatives to develop a singular definition of IFF, compare different IFF estimates, and develop a shared statistical framework through which to investigate the issue.

1.2.3 Flow

Most definitions associate the term "flow" with the concept of movement of capital (e.g., Clark, 2011; Global Initiative, 2018; Kar, 2010; World Bank, 2017), while others explicitly refer to the transnational transfer of money (e.g., Clark, 2011; World Bank, 2017). In fact, for most authors in the field, the transnational dimension of the phenomenon is as central as the illegitimacy of the practice; for example, according to the OECD (2014, 20), IFFs "are generated by methods, practices and crimes aiming to transfer financial capital out of a country in contravention of national or international laws." While other definitions fail to directly reference the transnational dimension of IFFs, the idea nevertheless emerges by virtue of their operationalization of the concept (e.g., Global Initiative, 2018; Kar, 2010).

However, the term "transfer" can be found in most definitions of IFFs together with the conjunction "or," which stands in contrast to "earn" and "utilize" (e.g., Global Initiative, 2018; Kar, 2010; World Bank, 2017). Here, the term "flows" can also take on the meaning of flows during a period of time (typically a year), in contrast to the concept of stock (the overall accumulation of IFFs) at a specific point in time. The available estimates, both by academics and institutions, invariably embrace both these positions, as they attempt to estimate transnational financial movements within a definite time span, rather than considering their overall accumulation (e.g., Hong & Pak, 2017; Janský & Kokeš, 2016; Kar & Cartwright-Smith, 2008; UNECA, 2015).

1.3 What Is Actually Meant by Illicit Financial Flows?

IFF has at its core the concept of (1) transnational transfers of assets that are (2) related to illegitimate activities in their generation, transfer, and use phases, even if an overarching consensus on conceptual and definitional issues related to the term IFFs has yet to be reached. Even if one agrees with this overview of the current state of play, the question of what IFFs actually are still remains to be answered. Or, phrased otherwise, what does the definition of IFF actually refer to? Does it refer to whether the generation, transfer, and use phases are illegitimate or the manner in which the three phases combine? Or does it concern the transfer methods that are related to IFFs? In practice, IFFs range from something as simple as a private individual evading taxes and transferring funds into private accounts abroad to highly complex systems set in place by criminal networks to hide their capital through the creation of multilevel multi-jurisdictional ownership schemes.

To aid the attempt to conceptualize IFFs, I propose a schematization of transnational movements of capital in relation to different combinations of the three key aspects present in most working definitions of IFF: capital generation legitimacy, international transaction legitimacy, and final use legitimacy. An IFF occurs whenever one or more of these three aspects are in some manner illegitimate and the involved assets are moved abroad. The following subsections hone in on the other cardinal concept within definitions of IFF, the transnational dimension. There, I describe the principal channels and methods that are used to move money out of a country illegally. Accounting for the conceptual differences between the generation, transfer, and use phases is of critical relevance for gaining a better understanding of IFF and in terms of being able to operationalize it in a more meaningful manner.

1.3.1 The Illegitimacy of the Related Activities

1.3.1.1 The Generation Phase

Money or other financial assets generated through illicit activities that are moved across borders constitute the first aspect of IFFs. The generation phase can be considered illegitimate in three major respects. First is if the proceeds of transnational crimes and illegal markets, such as drug trafficking/dealing, firearms trafficking, and wildlife trafficking, underpin IFF. Certain authors also include crimes like trafficking in persons, human smuggling, or counterfeiting within this subcategory (e.g., Cobham & Janský, 2017a; Reuter, 2012). Thefts, extortions, kidnappings, frauds, bankruptcies, or other theft-related crimes which do not have an international dimension per se constitute the second subcategory. The third group of crimes concerns proceeds stemming from corruption and may include bribery, illicit enrichment, and embezzlement. This subdivision based on predicate offenses for IFFs is functional for their measurement, given that the estimates of the proceeds stemming from different crimes are underpinned by distinct methodologies.

The legitimacy of the adopted transaction schemes is irrelevant for the classification of these flows as IFFs. In the same manner, the final use of the illicit proceeds is also irrelevant to the purposes of labeling these flows as illicit. In Fig. 1.2, cases 1, 2, 3, and 4 all concern IFFs. It is instructive to think of a burglar who sends part of his loot to her/his relatives in a foreign country as an example of criminal behavior that would come under case 1. The same burglars smuggling cash procured as part of their criminal activities out of the country to their relatives would fall under case 2. Indeed, in this case, also the adopted transfer system is illicit (i.e., cash smuggling). With respect to case 3, all three phases are connected to illicit behaviors (e.g., firearms traffickers forging invoices to transfer their illicit proceeds to terrorist organizations). Finally, drug traffickers reinvesting their proceeds in an additional supply of drugs would be an example of case 4, in the sense that they do not rely on

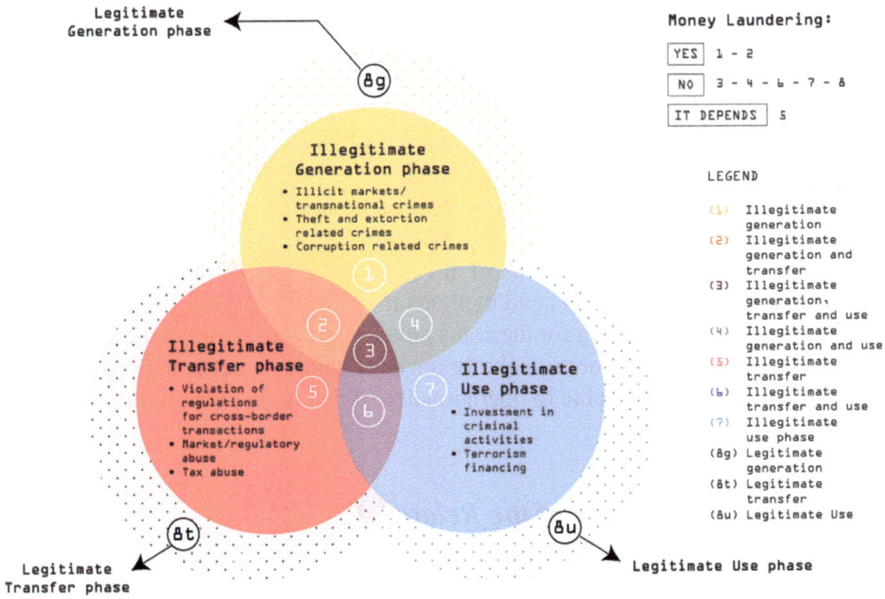

Fig. 1.2 Conceptual scheme for definition of illicit financial flows centered on the combination of the three phases: generation, transfer, and use.
Note: The most common working definitions of IFFs center on the concept of transnational financial transfers that are related to illegitimate activities in the generation, transfer, or use phases. IFF occurs whenever one or more of the three aspects are illegitimate and the assets move across borders. Seven out of eight possible combinations of the three phases concern IFFs – at least one of these three phases has an illicit dimension. Each of these combinations includes heterogeneous cases and can be subdivided further when analyzing practices in the real world. In contrast, the remaining combination of capital generation, transaction, and use is fully legitimate, because they are obtained through legal practices that are fully tax compliant and are legally transferred abroad for a legal purpose. The scheme underlines that the connection between IFFs and ML centers on the legitimacy/illegitimacy use of the assets. With respect to ML, then, it is particularly case 5, in which the illegitimacy is in the transfer phase rather than in the generation phase, and the predicate offenses for laundering are white-collar crimes, such as tax fraud and tax evasion. (Source: author's elaboration)

illegitimate money transfer methods. Of course, not all of these forms of IFF are related to ML, given that the use phase may also be illegitimate in nature; alternatively, the final use of the assets could concern the laundering (i.e., cases 1 and 2) or the illicit use of the proceeds of crime (i.e., in cases 3 and 4, the money could be used to finance terrorist activities or could be invested in further criminal activities).

The proceeds of criminal activities do not constitute IFF if there is no transnational movement of assets, according to the common definition of IFFs. This could happen in two respects. First is if criminals consume their proceeds as opposed to laundering them. Directly consuming proceeds typically occurs in the case of small-scale drug dealers or receivers of petty briberies, whose illicit earnings do not warrant subsequent investment (Levitt & Venkatesh, 2000; Reuter, 2017). Second is if criminals launder their money in their own country. Scholars have observed, for example, how laundering money in the local economy is a recurrent strategy of mafia-type organized criminal groups. By investing money in their own territory, organized crime members are able to strengthen their consensus, display their status, and control a particular market of the local economy; moreover, this choice is deemed to be easier and in certain respects safer due to insufficient financial skills (Savona and Berlusconi, 2015; Sciarrone, 2009).

1.3.1.2 The Transfer Phase

The combinations that center on the illegitimacy of the transaction phase constitute the second class of IFFs (i.e., case 5 – only the transfer phase is related to an illicit dynamic – but also cases 2, 3, and 6 in which the generation or use phase may also be related to illicit activities). Here, it is the manner in which the assets are moved across countries and the purpose of the movement which are the focal point of the classification. Paying close attention to the transfer phase demonstrates that IFF can take place with capital whose generation and final use can be placed anywhere on a spectrum of legality (Cobham, 2014). In many cases, the activities that generate the funds are wholly legitimate, the methods of transfer are legitimate per se (e.g., wire transfers, invoices), and their final use is legal, but the purpose and manner behind the capital movement ultimately make it illegitimate (i.e., case 5). The predicate offenses that determine the illegitimacy of the transfer phase are typically white-collar crimes, as opposed to the generation phase which is more characterized by "hard" crimes.

Legitimately generated funds can become IFFs if their movement violates regulations for cross-border transactions, such as evading currency controls. Market and regulatory abuses, which concern the circumvention of regulations on offshore ownership, can also be associated with IFFs. Finally, the broadest subcategory of practices that are included in this group concerns those movements connected with tax crimes or with other illegitimate fiscal practices, which are considered to be the most ubiquitous component of IFFs globally, and with respect to most individual countries in the world (Cobham & Loretz, 2014; OECD, 2014). The range of factors impacting upon the transfer phase cannot be comprehensive, due to the fact that the domain of illegitimate motivations is broad, and there is the potential to engineer an IFF within any transaction (Cobham, 2014).

Moreover, the reality of the situation is more ambiguous and complex than any proposed classification system can account for, and there is an entire spectrum of possibilities between one case and another, especially as it pertains to tax reduction practices (Cobham, 2014). Whether one should consider proceeds of tax evasion in the same way as one does the proceeds of a crime (they should be included in case 1 or 2 depending on their transfer method in the proposed scheme) or exclusively in terms of how capital is moved around the globe (they should go under case 5) is complex and may vary from case to case. Ultimately, the choice should depend on the role of the transfer phase in the tax abuse scheme. However, as aforesaid, the purpose of the analysis itself, its geographical scope, the availability of information, the researcher's sensibility about the topic, and her/his interpretation of IFF also play a significant role. Given that conceptual and classification choices can drastically impact on estimates, it is imperative that one critically interrogates and clarifies every decision when assessing IFFs.

1.3.1.3 The Use Phase

The third group of IFFs includes all those transactions that cross the border with the express purpose of committing illegal activities, such as the financing of terrorism or investments in illicit trafficking, irrespective of the origin of the funds or of the transfer mechanisms used. The use of illicit capital for these specific purposes automatically designates it as IFF, regardless of the other two elements of the analysis. Of course, it is wholly possible that capital licitly earned finds its way to a terrorist organization via charity (case 7). Alternatively, a criminal group could transfer abroad, through both licit (case 4) and illicit (case 3) means, its proceeds generated through illegal activities to fund further crimes. While these schemes are different in terms of their generation and transferring phases, they are all IFFs because the final use of the transferred money is illicit. For the same reason, none of these cases is linked to any ML activity.

The attention granted to this specific class of IFFs grew after the 9/11 attacks in New York and Washington, D.C. and the subsequent interest in international terrorism and its global financing mechanisms. Since then, the international community has developed legislation to prevent the flow of resources to and from terrorist organizations, such as the UN Security Council Resolution 1373 and the Financial Action Task Force's "FATF Special Recommendations on Terrorist Financing" (Krieger & Meierrieks, 2013).

1.3.2 The Transnational Dimension: Channels and Methods

The conceptualization of IFFs and their statistical measuring is complicated by the fact that IFFs are differentiated, not only according to the illegitimacy of the generation, transfer, and use phases but also according to the methods exploited to move capital abroad. The available means of transfer are more voluminous than the categories of IFFs themselves; indeed, criminals can exploit a wide range of movable assets from jewelry to artifacts, hide crime proceeds in complicit jurisdictions, alongside buy real estate in third countries, and use many other strategies, which makes it difficult to track IFFs (Reuter, 2017).

Among all the possible channels to transfer assets, some are more likely to be connected with certain predicate offenses than others (Reuter, 2013; Reuter & Truman, 2004). Cryptocurrencies, for example, are particularly used by criminals providing illicit goods and services via the darknet, a classification of Internet websites that requires the use of IP-obscuring web browsers to gain access (Janze, 2017). In the same manner, cash-intensive crimes like drug dealing and drug trafficking are more likely to exploit ML schemes based on cash (Riccardi & Levi, 2018; Soudijn and Reuter, 2016). At the same time, IFFs connected to different crimes may exploit the exact same channel. The same cryptocurrencies, for example, are also exploited in ransomware, and, indeed, there is growing evidence that they have been used to fund terrorist attacks (Brill & Keene, 2014; Irwin & Milad, 2016).

Finally, the proceeds of a single crime can be moved abroad through a variety of methods as shown in Fig. 1.3. This is the case of frauds (e.g., cash smuggling, reliance on shell companies, electronic transfers), proceeds from corruption (e.g., cash smuggling, reliance on shell companies), drug trafficking (e.g., trade-based ML techniques, cash smuggling), and other forms of illicit activities (GFI, 2015; Levi, 2013; Reuter, 2017). To design an estimation strategy capable of accounting for the intricate combinations of various sources of IFFs and the manifold means of transfer available is especially difficult. Given that the transnational shift of capital is a prerequisite of any IFF, gaining an accurate understanding of the numerous channels available to transfer capital should be a prerequisite for any statistical reasoning. With this in mind, the following subsections examine the most relevant transfer methods.

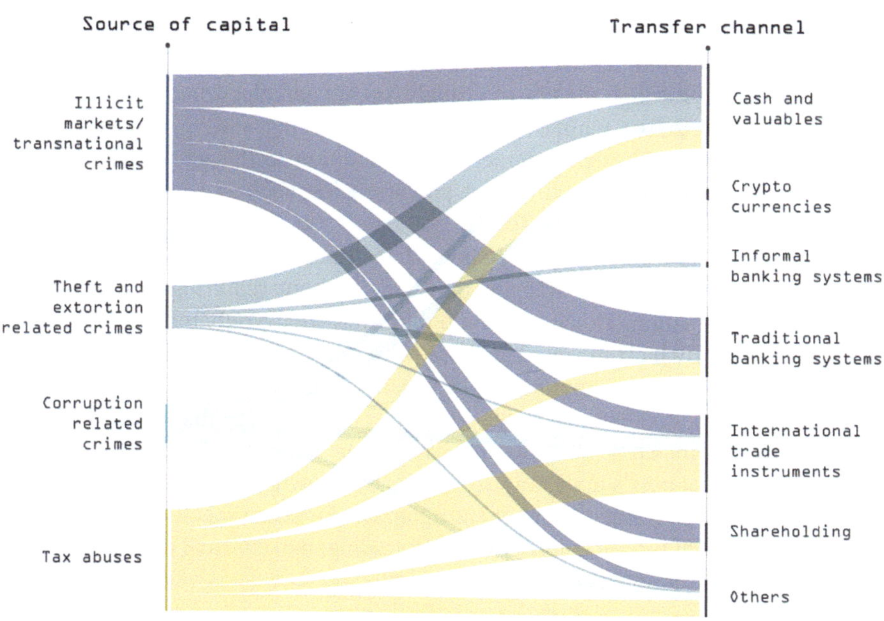

Fig. 1.3 Predicate offenses and methods of transfer: an intricate relationship.
Note: Predicate offenses and methods of transfer do not have a univocal relationship. While the proceeds of certain crimes are more likely to be moved through exploiting certain methods (e.g., drug trafficking and cash), ultimately multiple combinations are possible. (Source: author's elaboration)

1.3.2.1 Cash and Valuables

The physical smuggling of cash is one of the oldest placement techniques; to this day, both scholars and anti-money laundering/terrorist financing units around the world consider it to be the most frequently used method in suspicious transfers and as playing a central role in global ML (Riccardi & Levi, 2018; Soudijn and Reuter, 2016). The principal advantage of cash over other transfer methods is straightforward: cash is anonymous and hard to trace. Cash is a bearer negotiable instrument par excellence, which provides no information either to the origin of the capital or the beneficiary of the exchange (Riccardi & Levi, 2018). Soudijn and Reuter (2016), based on a series of case studies examining drug flows from Colombia to the Netherlands, observe that cocaine traffickers pay brokers to move their revenues from one country to the other by physically moving banknotes. Scholars have observed similar schemes of bulk cash smuggling with respect to other crimes, such as human smuggling, tax evasion, and the financing of terrorism (Cassella, 2004; Reuter & Truman, 2004). Precious commodities such as gems and antiquities – especially gold – have similar features and are thus also used to transfer illicit money by serving as "quasi-cash" (FATF, 2003; Riccardi & Levi, 2018).

1.3.2.2 Cryptocurrencies

Alongside traditional cash smuggling, technological advancements provide criminals with new opportunities to distance themselves and their assets from their illegal activities, such as through the use of virtual banking and electronic money transfer systems (Tropina, 2016). Online markets allow for buying, selling, and exchanging illicit goods without physical interactions. In addition to this, many platforms in operation on the darknet use virtual cryptocurrencies, such as Bitcoin or Monero, offer one particularly attractive feature for those seeking to move crime-related assets across countries: anonymity (Choo, 2015; Kethineni, Cao, & Dodge, 2017). Cryptocurrencies permit the transfer of values without requiring any personally identifiable information. This is because public keys are the only tool through which to identify users, which means that those who want to deanonymize users must rebuild the one-to-many mapping between users and public keys and then associate users with information external to the system. The technology that underpins many cryptocurrencies impedes recognition by storing the mapping of a user to her or his public keys on that user's node only, as well as by allowing each user to generate as many public keys as needed (Reid & Harrigan, 2013). These specific designs, allied with the substantial lack of control over their trading, make virtual cryptocurrencies an attractive tool for concealing illicit earnings.

1.3.2.3 Informal Banking Systems (IBS)

For centuries, alternative remittance or informal value transfer, also referred to as hawala, hundi, and fei chien in different parts of the world, has existed alongside traditional financial service providers to move funds from one geographical area to another (Buehn & Schneider, 2013; FATF, 2003). Hawala bankers collect cash, or other valuables in one country, and through their business partners pay a corresponding sum in another country (van de Bunt, 2008). To this day, millions of migrants, in particular Pakistanis and Indians, use these systems to send remittances to their relatives (Reuter, 2013). Since IBS generally operate outside traditional financial regulatory structures and thus circumvent the official recording system, criminals often exploit them to move criminal proceeds and to finance terrorism (FATF, 2003; Kar & Cartwright-Smith, 2008).

1.3.2.4 Traditional Banking System (TBS)

The traditional banking system is ordinarily less opaque than informal value transfer services; however, SWIFT and other regulated electronic transfer mechanisms that are used on a daily basis by millions of people can be connected to IFFs. TBS provides the possibility to move funds through several banks and different jurisdictions, which, in turn, makes it hard to trace the money and spot its illicit origins. The capillarity and efficiency of modern banking systems mean that money is readily available whenever and wherever it is needed. With respect to these features, authors have noted that the TBS is crucial for IFFs and a primary tool for ML practices (Buehn & Schneider, 2013). Notorious kleptocrats, such as Sani Abacha in Nigeria, Vladimiro Montesinos in Peru, or Ferdinand Marcos in the Philippines, all exploited the traditional banking system to secure profits stemming from a vast network of corruption practices. The money was ordinarily moved by common means, such as wire transfers, by complicit banks (OECD, 2014).

1.3.2.5 International Trade Instruments

Companies can exploit transfer mispricing, also known as trade mispricing, transfer pricing manipulation, and abusive transfer pricing, and trade misinvoicing (and multiple invoicing) to illicitly transfer money in different countries. These two classes of methods are among the principal conduits for the transfer of IFFs, especially in developing countries (APG, 2012; Baker, 2005). In trade mispricing, multinational enterprises exploit their organizational structure and the international scope of their operations to protect their profits from taxation, thus arbitraging and taking advantage of differences in taxation and regulations between countries (Eden, 2012). The mode of moving money across countries is based on the manipulation of prices of cross-border transactions between related affiliates. Price manipulation is particularly straightforward in the case of transferring of business-specific intangible assets, whose prices are especially difficult to determine. Multinational companies can lower their tax base in their host country, by moving intangible intermediate assets to low-tax countries (Dischinger & Riedel, 2011).

Unlike transfer price manipulation, transfer misinvoicing involves transactions between unrelated parties. Transfer misinvoicing either enables the movement of profits out of a country through import over-invoicing or through export under-invoicing (Hollingshead, 2010). Individuals and companies can thus collude with an unrelated party abroad to transfer money between countries by falsifying prices on a customs invoice (Forstater, 2018). The import over-invoicing and the export under-invoicing are not only used to escape taxation but also allow a resident to acquire foreign assets and move money internationally in a quick and hidden manner (Kar & Cartwright-Smith, 2008). The exploitation of trade misinvoicing is made simpler yet still by the fact that trading parties produce their own trade documents or have their documents prepared in a third country (typically a tax haven), a method known as re-invoicing (Kar & Spanjers, 2015).

1.3.2.6 Shareholding

Criminals may exploit ad hoc registered companies and offshore companies located in tax havens for money laundering (Riccardi & Savona, 2013; Unger et al., 2013), concealing grand corruption schemes (van der Does de Willebois, Halter, Harrison, Park, & Sharman, 2011), and tax evasion purposes (Janský & Kokeš, 2016). The typical process of such a scheme involves, firstly, establishing a company for a legitimate and fictitious commercial purpose. In the second stage, the owners mix their illicit proceeds with profits generated from their legal commercial activities. Ordinarily, various fraudulent accounting practices are required to succeed in this operation. A further way through which to obscure a company's true intent involves exploiting various additional offshore entities so that assets can be moved (FATF, 2003).

1.4 Conclusion

The utility of IFF stems from its ability to put a name to a complex phenomenon, chiefly the transnational transfer of money related to illicit activities. Indeed, if one does not wish to examine in more depth what precisely comes under the rubric of IFFs, then the term is an expedient one. However, problems soon occur when one wants to be more specific about what activities constitute IFF or if one seeks to develop accurate measures for the concept and, in turn, aid policymakers in designing interventions to combat the related issues. As this chapter has demonstrated, IFFs comprise of a range of phenomena connected to manifold forms of crimes, ranging from tax evasion to racketeering and human trafficking. At the same time,

IFFs exploit simple transfer means, such as cash smuggling, but also rely on complex misinvoicing schemes or the exploitation of providers of financial services located in tax heavens. Finally, IFFs also differ in respect to their economic nature. Some IFFs are connected to trades in the real economy; others are untied from physical transactions. A payment due for the purchase of an illegal service (e.g., illicit waste management) or good (e.g., a drug load) is an example of IFFs; transfers whose express purpose is to reduce tax liability are also considered to be IFFs; and movements aimed toward laundering money, which are already illicit or used to fund terrorist activities, are also examples of IFFs.

Greater attention should be dedicated to the actual ends of monitoring IFFs. Scholars have observed that the fight against transnational ML has different purposes whose relative relevance is ultimately subjective: the reduction of predicate offenses, such as corruption, tax evasion, and transnational crimes, the fight against kleptocracies and terrorism, and safeguarding the international financial system (Lagarde, 2017; Reuter, 2013). Controlling and combating IFFs are of even greater importance, given that the concept of IFF is broader than that of ML. Indeed, the heterogeneity of the scenarios and behavior that encompass the term IFF itself is such that one must call into question the current utility and meaningfulness of the term and seek to develop it in a manner more capable of accounting for this aforesaid heterogeneity.

The challenges are not strictly limited to the semantic and theoretical conceptualization of the phenomena but also concern the development of accurate estimation strategies. Here, the question becomes how would it be possible to estimate a phenomenon that is so heterogeneous, multifaceted, and flexible? Adopting a conceptual definition of IFFs, which combines that which can be considered definitively illegal with that which is uncertain because it is deemed to be detrimental by some group, only serves to muddy the waters further and make it harder to produce and compare estimates. Of course, disputes around definitions and semantic analyses may be perceived as a distraction from developing effective interventions, but as Forstater (2018) notes, dissenting and inaccurate language can ultimately obstruct understanding and constructive dialogue.

Current theoretical doxa embraces deeply different phenomena, whose countering measures need to be specific in order to be effective. Consequently, is it expedient to clump together profit shifting, laundering of bribes, and payments of drug loads that are potentially based on wholly distinct transfer methods? This is problematic if one believes that estimations of IFFs should differentiate at least between the generation, transfer, and use phases, so as to generate more meaningful and specific policy recommendations. This is especially the case from a criminological perspective, where I advocate a shift from the concept of IFFs to the concept of "IFF related to" in the sense that IFFs should be always related to something specific to assume an actual meaning. We should refer to IFF related to a specific source of capital, a specific method of transfer, or a specific illegitimate use rather than generically refer to IFFs. At the risk of losing scope and elegance, the use of the term IFF should become more narrowly defined to transform in a useful instrument to understand and contrast the economic side of criminal activities.

Today, conceptual and practical issues are so severe that "we have no methodology that plausibly would produce credible numbers. [...] What I hope to persuade you of is that there is no prospect, either in surveys of experts or in studies of crimes themselves as reflected in criminal justice statistics, for developing persuasive estimates" (Reuter, 2013, 224), given the broadness of current definitions of IFFs. While this assertion may well be true, it should not preclude theorizing about how to estimate what we can actually estimate, which data we can begin to collect in order to improve our estimates, which would be one feasible means through which to estimate flows that hitherto we are unable to measure.

Indeed, despite these challenges, the necessity for accurately measuring IFFs is clear, as one can discern from the IFF estimation fever which has spread in recent years. Researchers have developed several methods for assessing the dimensions of IFFs, which differ with respect to how they frame the problem. This is important because policymakers and activists rely on these estimates of IFFs to gauge their seriousness and advocate for interventions to solve the issue. Finally, for economic development programs, there is an urgent need for baselines against which progress of initiatives to address the problem can be measured. The next chapter provides an overview of the main methodologies, clarifies the different aspects of the problem covered by each model, and discusses their key limitations.

References

APG. (2012). *Trade based money laundering*. Sydney: Asia/Pacific Group on Money Laundering http://www.fatf-gafi.org/media/fatf/documents/reports/Trade_Based_ML_APGReport.pdf

Baker, R. W. (2005). *Capitalism's Achilles heel: Dirty money and how to renew the free-market system* (1st ed.). Hoboken, NJ: Wiley.

Baker, R. W. (2015). A brief biography of illicit financial flows. In D. Kar, R. W. Baker, & T. Cardamone (Eds.), *Illicit financial flows: The most damaging economic condition facing the developing world* (pp. 1–5). Washington, DC: Global Financial Integrity http://www.gfintegrity.org/report/illicit-financial-flows-damaging-economic-problem-facing-developing-world/

Barakat, S. (2008). *Reconstructing Post-Saddam Iraq*. London: Routledge.

Blankenburg, S., & Khan, M. (2012). Governance and illicit flows. In P. H. Reuter (Ed.), *Draining development? Controlling flows of illicit funds from developing countries* (pp. 21–68). Washington, DC: The World Bank http://documents.worldbank.org/curated/en/305601468178737192/Draining-development-Controlling-flows-of-illicit-funds-from-developing-countries

Brill, A., & Keene, L. (2014). Cryptocurrencies: The next generation of terrorist financing? In *SSRN scholarly paper ID 2814914*. Rochester, NY: Social Science Research Network https://papers.ssrn.com/abstract=2814914

Buehn, A., & Schneider, F. (2013). A preliminary attempt to estimate the financial flows of transnational crime using the MIMIC method. In B. Unger & D. van der Linde (Eds.), *Research handbook on money laundering* (pp. 172–182). Edward Elgar Publishing.

Cassella, S. D. (2004). Bulk cash smuggling and the globalization of crime: Overcoming constitutional challenges to forfeiture under 31 U.S.C. 5332. *Berkeley Journal of International Law, 22*, 98.

Choo, K.-K. R. (2015). Cryptocurrency and virtual currency: Corruption and money laundering/terrorism financing risks? In D. L. K. Chuen (Ed.), *Handbook of digital currency* (pp. 283–307). San Diego: Academic Press.

Clark, H. (2011). Clark: Illicit finances divert resources away from development. United Nations Development Programme. http://www.undp.org/content/undp/en/home/presscenter/speeches/2011/05/11/clark-illicit-finances-divert-resources-away-from-development.html

Cobham, A. (2014). The impact of illicit financial flows (IFFs) on peace and security in Africa. Tana High-Level Forum on Security in Africa. http://www.tanaforum.org/y-file-store/Discussion_Papers/2014/iscussionillicit_financial_flows_conflict_and_security_in_africal.pdf

Cobham, A., & Janský, P. (2017a). Illicit financial flows: An overview. UNCTAD. http://unctad.org/meetings/en/SessionalDocuments/tdb_efd1_bp_CJ_en.pdf

Cobham, A., & Janský, P. (2017b). Measuring misalignment: The location of US multinationals' economic activity versus the location of their profits. *Development Policy Review, 48*, 1–48.

Cobham, A., & Loretz, S. (2014). "International distribution of the corporate tax base: Implications of different apportionment factors under unitary taxation. SSRN scholarly paper ID 2587839. Rochester, NY: Social Science Research Network. https://papers.ssrn.com/abstract=2587839

Dischinger, M., & Riedel, N. (2011). Corporate taxes and the location of intangible assets within multinational firms. *Journal of Public Economics, 95*(7), 691–707.

Dorling, D., Gordon, D., Hillyard, P., Pantazis, C., Pemberton, S., & Tombs, S. (2008). Criminal obsessions: Why harm matters more than crime. https://ora.ox.ac.uk/objects/uuid:ba62580b-78ee-4726-ac39-78ca220e5c8d

Eden, L. (2012). Transfer price manipulation. In P. H. Reuter (Ed.), *Draining development? Controlling flows of illicit funds from developing countries* (pp. 205–233). Washington, DC: The World Bank http://documents.worldbank.org/curated/en/305601468178737192/Draining-development-Controlling-flows-of-illicit-funds-from-developing-countries

Epstein, G. A. (2005). *Capital flight and capital controls in developing countries*. Cheltenham: Edward Elgar Publishing.

FATF. (2003). *Money laundering typologies 2002-2003*. Paris: Financial Action Task Force on Money Laundering http://www.fatf-gafi.org/media/fatf/documents/reports/2002_2003_ML_Typologies_ENG.pdf

Forstater, M. (2018). Illicit financial flows, trade misinvoicing, and multinational tax avoidance: The same or different? 123. CGD policy paper. Washington, DC: Center for Global Development. https://www.cgdev.org/publication/illicit-financial-flows-trade-misinvoicing-and-multinational-tax-avoidance

GFI. (2015). Illicit financial flows. Global Financial Integrity. 2015. http://www.gfintegrity.org/issue/illicit-financial-flows/

Global Initiative. (2018). Illicit financial flows. The Global Initiative Against Transnational Organized Crime. 2018. http://globalinitiative.net/programs/financial/

Hollingshead, A. (2010). *The implied tax revenue loss from trade mispricing*. Washington, DC: Global Financial Integrity http://www.gfintegrity.org/storage/gfip/documents/reports/implied%20tax%20revenue%20loss%20report_final.pdf

Hong, K. P., & Pak, S. J. (2017). Estimating trade misinvoicing from bilateral trade statistics: the devil is in the details. *The International Trade Journal, 31*(1), 3–28.

Irwin, A. S. M., & Milad, G. (2016). The use of crypto-currencies in funding violent jihad. *Journal of Money Laundering Control, 19*(4), 407–425.

Janský, P., & Kokeš, O. (2016). Profit-shifting from Czech multinational companies to European tax havens. *Applied Economics Letters, 23*(16), 1130–1133.

Janze, C. (2017). Are cryptocurrencies criminals best friends? Examining the co-evolution of bitcoin and darknet markets. In AMCIS 2017 proceedings. http://aisel.aisnet.org/amcis2017/InformationSystems/Presentations/2

Kar, D. (2010). Illicit financial flows from developing countries: The absurdity of traditional methods of estimation. Global Financial Integrity. http://www.gfintegrity.org/illicit-financial-flows-from-developing-countries-the-absurdity-of-traditional-methods-of-estimation/

Kar, D., & Cartwright-Smith, D. (2008). *Illicit financial flows from developing countries: 2002–2006*. Washington, DC: Global Financial Integrity http://www.gfintegrity.org/storage/gfip/executive%20-%20final%20version%201-5-09.pdf

Kar, D., & Spanjers, J. (2015). *Illicit financial flows from developing countries: 2004-2013*. Washington, DC: Global Financial Integrity http://www.gfintegrity.org/report/illicit-financial-flows-from-developing-countries-2004-2013/

Kethineni, S., Cao, Y., & Dodge, C. (2017). Use of bitcoin in darknet markets: Examining facilitative factors on bitcoin-related crimes. *American Journal of Criminal Justice*, 1–17.

Krieger, T., & Meierrieks, D. (2013). Terrorism: Causes, effects and the role of money laundering. In B. Unger & D. van der Linde (Eds.), *Research handbook on money laundering* (pp. 78–91). Edward Elgar Publishing.

Lagarde, C. 2017. Working together to fight money laundering & terrorist financing. presented at the IMF managing director FATF plenary meeting, Valencia. https://www.imf.org/en/News/Articles/2017/06/21/sp062217-working-together-to-fight-money-laundering-terrorist-financing

Levi, M. (2013). The costs of fraud. In B. Unger & D. van der Linde (Eds.), *Research handbook on money laundering* (pp. 68–77). Edward Elgar Publishing.

Levitt, S. D., & Venkatesh, S. A. (2000). An economic analysis of a drug-selling Gang's finances. *The Quarterly Journal of Economics, 115*(3), 755–789.

Melzer, S. A. (2010). *Counterfeit and contraband cigarette smuggling: Opportunities, actors, and guardianship*. Washington, DC: American University http://gradworks.umi.com/34/17/3417880.html

OECD. (2000). *The fight against bribery and corruption*. Paris: OECD http://www.oecd.org/governance/ethics/1918235.pdf

OECD. (2014). *Illicit financial flows from developing countries: Measuring OECD responses*. Paris: Organisation for Economic Co-operation and Development - OECD https://www.oecd.org/corruption/Illicit_Financial_Flows_from_Developing_Countries.pdf

Picciotto, S. (2007). Constructing compliance: Game playing, tax law, and the regulatory state. *Law & Policy, 29*(1), 11–30.

Picciotto, S. (2011). *Regulating global corporate capitalism*. Cambridge/New York: Cambridge University Press.

Reid, F., & Harrigan, M. (2013). An analysis of anonymity in the bitcoin system. In *Security and privacy in social networks* (pp. 197–223). New York, NY: Springer.

Reuter, P. H. (2017). *Illicit financial flows and governance: The importance of disaggregation*. Washington, DC: World Bank http://pubdocs.worldbank.org/en/677011485539750208/WDR17-BP-Illicit-Financial-Flows.pdf

Reuter, P. H. (2013). Are estimates of the volume of money laundering either feasible or useful? In B. Unger & D. van der Linde (Eds.), *Research handbook on money laundering* (pp. 224–232). Edward Elgar Publishing.

Reuter, P. H. (2012). *Draining development? controlling flows of illicit funds from developing countries*. 66815. The World Bank. http://documents.worldbank.org/curated/en/305601468178737192/Drainingdevelopment-Controlling-flows-of-illicit-funds-from-developing-countries

Reuter, P. H., & Truman, E. M. (2004). *Chasing dirty money: The fight against money laundering*. Washington, DC: Institute for International Economics.

Riccardi, M., & Levi, M. (2018). Cash, crime and anti-money laundering. In C. King, C. Walker, & G. Jimmy (Eds.), The Palgrave handbook of criminal and terrorism financing law, Colin King: Springer; Basingstoke, UK: Palgrave Macmillan. www.springer.com/us/book/9783319644974

Riccardi, M., & Savona, E. U. (2013). *The identification of beneficial owners in the fight against money laundering*. Trento: Transcrime – Università degli Studi di Trento http://www.transcrime.it/pubblicazioni/the-identification-of-beneficial-owners-in-the-fight-against-money-laundering-2/

Savona, E. U., & Berlusconi, G. (2015). *Organized Crime Infiltration of Legitimate Businesses in Europe: A Pilot Project in Five European Countries. Final Report of Project ARIEL*. Trento: Transcrime – Università degli Studi di Trento.

Sciarrone, R. (2009). *Mafie vecchie, mafie nuove. Radicamento ed espansione*. Roma: Donzelli.

Soudijn, M., & Reuter, P. (2016). Cash and carry: The high cost of currency smuggling in the drug trade. *Crime, Law and Social Change, 66*(3), 271–290.

Steinberg, J. (2005). '*The Illicit Abalone Trade in South Africa*'. 105. Pretoria: Institute for Security Studies. https://issafrica.s3.amazonaws.com/site/uploads/105.PDF

Tropina, T. (2016). *Do Digital Technologies Facilitate Illicit Financial Flows?* Washington, DC: The World Bank. http://pubdocs.worldbank.org/en/396751453906608518/WDR16-BP-Do-Digital-Technologies-Facilitate-Illicit-Financial-Flows-Tropina.pdf

UNECA. (2015). *Illicit Financial Flows: Report of the High Level Panel on Illicit Financial Flows from Africa*. Addis Ababa: United Nations. Economic Commission for Africa (UN.ECA). http://repository.uneca.org/handle/10855/22695

Unger, B., Addink, H., Walker, J., Ferwerda, J., van den Broek, M., & Deleanu, I. (2013). *The Economic and Legal Effectiveness of Anti-Money Laundering and Combating Terrorist Financing Policy*. Utrecht: Utrecht University and the European Commission DG Home Affairs. http://www2.econ.uu.nl/users/unger/ecolef_files/Final%20ECOLEF%20report%20(digital%20version).pdf

UNODC/OECD. (2016). '*Coherent policies for combatting illicit financial flows*'. Issue Brief. United Nations Office on Drugs and Crime (UNODC)/Organisation for Economic Cooperation and Development (OECD). http://www.un.org/esa/ffd/wp-content/uploads/2016/01/Coherent-policies-for-combatting-Illicit-Financial-Flows_UNODC-OECD_IATF-Issue-Brief.pdf

van de Bunt, H. (2008). A case study on the misuse of hawala banking. *International Journal of Social Economics, 35*(9), 691–702.

van der Does de Willebois, E., Halter, E. M., Harrison, R. A., Park, J. W., & Sharman, J. C. (2011). *The puppet masters: How the corrupt use legal structures to hide stolen assets and what to do about it* (1st ed.). Washington, DC: World Bank Publications.

World Bank. (2017). '*Illicit Financial Flows (IFFs)*'. World Bank. 2017. http://www.worldbank.org/en/topic/financialsector/brief/illicit-financial-flows-iffs

Chapter 2
How Illicit Financial Flows Are Estimated

2.1 Introduction

There is still a relative dearth of literature on illicit financial flows (IFFs). In particular, notwithstanding anecdotal evidence and embryonic academic research, there is a clear lacuna in extant literature with respect to accurate scales and patterns of IFFs. In line with this, also the methodologies used for measuring the proceeds of crime and the attendant IFFs are at an early stage of development, and the systematization of the available methods and instruments that is required to accurately measure IFFs is itself still underdeveloped.

There is a range of issues involved with designing a sound methodology for the estimation of IFFs. The first difficulty pertains to the conceptual definition of IFFs, as various policy makers and stakeholders currently interpret this broad term in distinct ways. The second issue concerns the statistical feasibility of measuring IFFs. In general, the quantification of IFFs is especially challenging in light of the fact that not only are their underlying actions concealed or disguised, but they are also characterized by processes of financial secrecy so as to remain hidden from law enforcement authorities and regulators. Although, in the prior two decades, international institutions have increased the availability of data on illicit markets and on economic indicators related to IFFs, the statistical limitations nevertheless remain severe.

Researchers have hitherto estimated IFFs by either identifying anomalies in public data, tracing the channels through which illicit funds are transferred – top-down approaches – or, alternatively, focusing on the predicate offenses through which the illicit proceeds have been accumulated, bottom-up approach. To the best of the author's knowledge, estimates of IFFs based upon the final illicit use of the funds are entirely absent in extant literature. Scholars interested in economic development primarily attempt to estimate capital flight with respect to private households or via firm trade. For those scholars whose primary interest is money laundering (ML) and terrorism financing, they invariably perform unusual transaction analy-

A. Aziani, *Illicit Financial Flows*, SpringerBriefs in Criminology,
https://doi.org/10.1007/978-3-030-01890-0_2

ses. Finally, the *Walker Gravity Model* involves estimating the proceeds of predicate offenses and assessing the direction of their overseas movements. Despite the fact that these methods are associated with distinct disciplinary approaches with often different final aims, the purpose of this chapter is to provide a framework through which to understand the key features of the main IFF estimation procedures used in extant literature. It is hoped that the critical evaluation of these methodologies will contribute to the development of more effective empirical initiatives to estimate the extent of IFFs.

The chapter is structured as follows. The first section provides an overview of top-down measurements of IFFs that center on anomalies analyses, the transfer phase of illicit capital, and wealth held in offshore jurisdictions. The second section describes the main bottom-up approaches that are based on estimating the proceeds of crime and the analysis of ML behavior. The third section summarizes the common limitations of all these respective methodologies. The chapter ends with concluding remarks.

2.2 Top-Down Approaches

Anomaly-based estimations are the most prominent type of top-down approaches; these methods rely, in one way or another, on identifying incongruities in public data that may arise from the process of hiding illicit capital. More specifically, *capital account-based estimates* focus on anomalies in the recording of capital movements, while *trade-based* estimates analyze statistical discrepancies in current accounts (via mispriced trade). Researchers and institutions also exploit other methods, such as simultaneously analyzing financial and trade data or signals from fiscal intelligence units (i.e., suspicious or *unusual transaction analyses*); finally, other researchers are starting to concentrate on *offshore wealth estimates*. Top-down approaches ultimately aim to produce an overall estimate of IFFs, which is hard to subdivide according to different predicate offenses or illicit uses. However, given that some of these aforesaid methods (e.g., *offshore wealth estimates*, *mispriced trade estimates*, *unusual transaction analyses*) exploit data on specific transfer methods, they provide details about the transfer phase.

2.2.1 Capital Account-Based Estimates

The *hot money narrow* (HMN) and the *World Bank residual* (WBR) methods are the most commonly used *source-and-use* methods for estimating IFFs via observing capital account anomalies. The HMN method involves analyzing errors and omissions in the national balance of payments (BoP), which records all monetary transactions conducted between countries. In principle, within the national BoP, credits and debts should amount to zero, since funds going out or being used to pay debts should be compensated for by the funds that are received. In actuality, the two classes of funds do not precisely coincide. The underlying assumption of the HMN method is that what remains is IFFs (Kar & Cartwright-Smith, 2008). Fontana (2010) defines the HMN method as IFFs equal to all funds coming in (credit) minus all funds going out (debt). Different versions of the HMN method have been adopted by international organizations such as the UNDP (2011), nongovernmental organizations such as the Tax Justice Network (Henry, 2012), and academics in the field (e.g., Lensink, Hermes, & Murinde, 2000).

The principal idea behind the WBR is similar; the total funds used by a country are subtracted from the total funds entering that country, and, whenever more funds are coming in than are being used, the resulting shortfall is considered to be evidence of IFFs. Increases in net external indebtedness of the public sector and net inflow of foreign direct investments correspond to sources of funds, while all the current account deficits and additions to reserves pertain to the potential uses of the funds (de Boyrie, Pak, & Zdanowicz, 2005b; Kar & Cartwright-Smith, 2008).

Both the WBR and the HMN methods rely on anomalies in the BoP identity. However, the HMN method relies directly on the "net errors and omissions" line in the BoP, a "catch-all" category obtained by deducting the current account and the capital account from the financial account and focuses on flows that are short-term in nature. The WBR method instead calculates the discrepancy between the sources of funds and the uses of funds and takes into account both short-term and longer-term movements of capital (Lensink et al., 2000). By collecting raw data from each country and purposefully calculating the residuals without relying solely on the error line of the BoP, the WBR provides results which are likely more accurate than those obtained through the HMN method (Fontana, 2010). Nonetheless, there are several conceptual issues related to both the HMN and the WBR methods that need to be addressed.

As aforesaid, the estimates emerging from the HMN and the WBR approaches are dependent on assumptions about how best to interpret the observed asymmetries in official data; firstly in so doing, they run the risk of confounding these statistical anomalies, such as data errors and mismatches, due to timing and rounding up errors and to designate them as indicators of illicit activities (Fuest & Riedel, 2012; Hong & Pak, 2017; Nitsch, 2012). Secondly, source-and-use measurements of IFFs merge together both legitimate and illegitimate capital transfers. For example, to the extent that private households purchase foreign securities to diversify their investments, such flows of capital would also be included in estimates of IFFs. Any distinction between legitimate and illegitimate capital exports is based on partially arbitrary criteria, when one adopts a normative interpretation of IFFs. However, open and legal international money transfers driven by portfolio diversification currently lie outside any current definition of IFF (Johannesen & Pirttilä, 2016). Finally, by design, if perfect data were readily available on a given illicit flow, that flow would tend toward zero. Conversely, under-/overestimating current account deficits would lead to over-/underestimations of IFFs. At the same time, although capital account estimates provide negative estimates of IFFs, this is deemed to be not really meaningful (Cobham & Janský, 2017b; Johannesen & Pirttilä, 2016).

2.2.2 Trade-Based Estimates

Since the 1960s, economists have analyzed gaps in trade statistics to quantify capital flight and estimate levels of tax evasion (e.g., Bhagwati, 1964). To this day, a relevant class of models estimates transfer mispricing and trade misinvoicing, which the Global Financial Integrity (GFI) designates as the principal modes for international illicit money transfers (Kar & Spanjers, 2015). Transfer mispricing can be understood as an abuse of transfer pricing procedures used to deceive tax authorities or to manipulate markets by setting trading prices between related parties in an ad hoc manner. Trade misinvoicing refers to the deliberate misreporting of the value of a commercial transaction, the express purpose of which is to illicitly move money across borders. Unlike transfer mispricing, trade misinvoicing concerns transactions between unrelated parties. Ideally, trade-based methodologies would compare data at the trade level to highlight irregularities in the declared imports (or exports) of a company (Kar & Spanjers, 2015).

In reality, import and export trade data at the transactional level are ordinarily unavailable, especially with respect to intrafirm trade (Pak, 2012). Statistics on intrafirm trades are scarce because most countries do not require multinational enterprises to separate their reports on their transnational intrafirm transactions from their trade with unrelated parties (Eden, 2012). Therefore, researchers often shift their attention to country-level analyses, which, in turn, further reduces the precision of their estimates. Alternatively, using more detailed data about a single country for which a specific database is available often comes at the cost of reducing the scope of the estimates (Eden, 2012; Spanjers, 2015). Indeed, most of the studies that rely upon detailed trade data focus on the United States and Western European countries. Within this class of methods, the *abnormal pricing method* used by de Boyrie, Pak, and Zdanowicz (2005a) to study illicit flows between Russia and the United States exploits information on prices and quantities at the transactional level in order to estimate an exchange-price distribution for different product categories. Subsequently, the authors assume that price anomalies are, in fact, evidence of tampering with capital leaks.

Turning our attention to more aggregated data, researchers compare what a country claims to import from (or export to) the rest of the world with what the rest of the world states it exports to (or imports from) that given country. Alternatively, anomalies stemming from mispricing of transactions between both related and unrelated parties can be detected by looking at each single partner country (Spanjers, 2015). The most commonly exploited source of information for this purpose is the *Direction of Trade Statistics* (DOTS) database by the IMF (Fontana, 2010; Nicolaou-Manias & Wu, 2016). However, even when adopting this strategy, problems nevertheless remain because of the nature of the required data.

Authors that adopt anomaly-based approaches based on trade misinvoicing must contend with the fact that not all countries supply consistent bilateral trade data; and, moreover, when a host of countries do provide consistent bilateral trade data, it is unlikely to have bilateral data for all traded goods (Spanjers & Salomon, 2017).

An additional problem in the data required for anomaly-based estimates concerns time lags. Economic transactions take time to complete, and countries on either side of a transaction may record trade volumes in different years; nonetheless, top-down approaches do not take into account discrepancies stemming from time lags (Kar & Cartwright-Smith, 2008). Official agencies may convert trade data into US dollars at a different exchange rate than those that may have been adopted by the parties of that specific trade, which introduces another potential source of bias (Spanjers & Salomon, 2017). To mitigate these issues, researchers from the GFI, for example, assess the underlying data before producing their estimates of IFFs from developing countries. More specifically, they check if outflows with characteristics indicative of illicit practices remain consistent for at least 3 out of 5 years before considering them within their estimates. Nonetheless, the paucity of the underlying data limits the accuracy of the estimates of IFFs.

2.2.3 Combined Capital Account and Trade Approaches

Researchers also combine capital account and trade approaches to create composite estimates of IFFs. *Capital account and trade combined approaches* are designed to consider both funds that flow through the banking system and funds that flow through fraudulent invoices in import/export operations (Fontana, 2010). It is interesting to note here that the well-known GFI shifted from using the classic WBR method to the modified version, which takes into account trade misinvoicing (Kar, Cartwright-Smith, & Hollingshead, 2010). The current GFI approach thus combines capital account estimates with trade estimates (i.e., *trade misinvoicing* model) and makes further adjustments through a two-stage filtration process of non-normalized estimates (Spanjers & Salomon, 2017).

A strength of combining these two approaches is that it is free from overlaps, in the sense that combined models are capable of capturing data for different types of IFFs. Hence, the WBR might spot cases of internal misappropriation of public resources by identifying discrepancies between the source and use of official funds, while, by concentrating on the money lost through the artificial manipulation of the value of goods, trade misinvoicing might signal forms of tax evasion (Fontana, 2010; UNODC, 2011).

2.2.4 Suspicious or Unusual Transaction Analyses

Scrutinizing the *suspicious or unusual transactions* reported to and by financial intelligence units (FIUs), which are active in most countries to combat ML, is a further method for estimating IFFs. "A suspicious transaction is one for which there are reasonable grounds to suspect that the transaction is related to a ML offence or a terrorist activity financing offence" (FINTRAC, 2017, 1). A transaction might be labeled as suspicious for a number of reasons. For example, the transaction may exceed a certain threshold amount; it fails to match the customer's business needs; it may have an unnecessarily complicated structure; it involves the simultaneous opening of multiple bank accounts; or it may serve no apparent purpose (Blöker, 2003; FATF, 2010; Unger & van Waarden, 2009). The value of the signaled transaction works serves as a minimum proxy of IFFs; alternatively, the same value might be multiplied by a parameter representing the hypothesized fraction of illicit transfers that FIUs are capable of detecting.

To understand the relationship between the number of signals and the actual number or value of illicit transactions is not a straightforward task, as is the case with any indicator of law enforcement actions. Indeed, it might ultimately be impossible to both identify truly suspicious transactions among the overall volume of signals and estimate the ratio between signals and the actual number of illicit transactions. This is because increases in the number of signals about specific transactions may be due to both an actual increase in illicit transactions and procedural changes by the respective authorities. Indeed, the strategic dilution of information by respondents may culminate in biases; appointed officials from the FIUs may fear negative judgment of their work if they miss illicit transactions, thus inflating the number of signaled transactions (Dalla Pellegrina & Masciandaro, 2009). This issue has been confirmed by scholars who have shown that the signals considered useful for starting investigations have either fallen or remained low, despite the overall increase in transactions signaled by FIUs in several countries, such as Italy, the United Kingdom, or the United States. Therefore, counting suspicious transactions can lead to errors in two respects. Suspicious transactions can be false positives, i.e., transactions that are legitimate, while, similarly, transactions which have not been red-flagged may be false negatives, in the sense that they are, in fact, criminal.

Approaches that focus on the transfer channel, like the *unusual transactions analyses*, run the risk of double-counting IFFs. As the name itself denotes, it is during the generation phase that the funds are generated either legally or illegally; it is this figure that eventually culminates in IFFs. In contrast, during the transfer, phase money does not increase, but, rather, it moves. Dozens of transactions through different channels take place within and between countries during the laundering and transfer processes, but the illicit amount generated through any given crime does not change. Hence, even if one focuses on a single method, it is impossible to exclude any double counting, as multiple transactions can take place through the same channel. In contrast, estimates that focus on a single channel will miss those transactions that are based on alternative transfer methods (Walker & Unger, 2013).

The more countries one includes in the analysis, the more ramified and complex the actual financial system behind IFFs becomes, and the larger the potential bias due to multiple counting. Not only will illicit money pass through multiple financial institutions within a given country, it will also do the same from country to country. Although we could consider each of these additional transactions as an illicit flow per se, the final estimates emerging from the sum of all these steps would not be the most significant ones from which to design better crime reduction or economic development policies. The impact of IFFs is much stronger on the country from where the money originally exits or where it finally ends; the spillovers are usually less affecting for the jurisdictions through which the capital transits.

2.2.5 *Offshore Wealth and Flow Estimates*

Finally, a pioneering stream of research proposes that we should estimate the scale of IFFs by assessing the stock of capital held in tax havens (Alstadsæter, Johannesen, & Zucman, 2017). Firstly, this approach uses data on international assets and liability positions to identify particular jurisdictions with anomalous situations. One adherent of this approach, Zucman (2013), focused on a group of tax havens, more specifically, the potential undeclared wealth that was held in these locations. Secondly, whenever country-level estimates are available, it becomes possible to use the stocks of potential undeclared wealth held in offshore accounts as a means to estimate the income streams that accrued it. *Offshore wealth estimates* provide estimates of IFFs with a high degree of uncertainty, given the data which is currently available. Indeed, on top of the errors that emerge when estimating the wealth held offshore, the additional extrapolations – from outflows to stocks and then to potential income streams – only serve to exacerbate the potential margin of error (Cobham & Janský, 2017a).

2.3 Bottom-Up Approach Focusing on the Generation Phase: The Walker Gravity Model

The *Walker Gravity Model* (WGM) is unique among the panorama of strategies for estimating IFFs, as it is the sole approach to estimating IFFs that begins from analyzing the proceeds of crime, not to mention that it relies on a risk assessment. Walker (1995, 1999, 2007) and his colleagues – e.g., Walker and Unger (2009, 2013) – designed this approach to produce macro estimates of the global extent of ML. According to the authors, the same strategy can be adapted to also assess the scale of IFFs (UNODC, 2011).

The WGM involves three main steps. First, it requires an estimation of the proceeds of all those crimes which may generate IFFs (i.e., transnational crimes and illicit markets, theft and extortion-related crimes, corruption-related crimes) within single countries around the world. Second, it is necessary to estimate the probability that those proceeds are laundered internationally. Third, a risk assessment gravity model is developed to map the flow of illicit capital between any potential pair of countries (UNODC, 2011; Walker & Unger, 2009). Gravity models take inspiration from Newton's universal law of gravity, in that attraction between two objects depends on the mass of these objects and (the inverse of) their squared mutual distance. Within the WGM framework, then, the volume of illicit flows between countries increases depending on the specific risk and opportunities that are associated with the financial sectors/institutions in each country, such as banking secrecy, economic size, level of corruption, and geographical and cultural distance.

Different scholars have raised a number of criticisms with respect to the model conceptualized by Walker and his colleagues (Fontana, 2010; Reuter, 2013). Most of these critiques concern the calculi on which it relies and the data that it relies upon. Reuter (2013), for example, purports that the results of WGMs are characterized by a series of inconsistencies in the proposed intermediate estimates compared with other literature in the field. Specifically, with respect to the illicit market for psychoactive substances, doubts persist about Walker's assumptions and calculi regarding the number of consumers, per year consumption of drugs, and the percentage of revenues from drug sales that are laundered.

WGM faces problems with respect to the accuracy of national statistics that are required to estimate the proceeds of crime. Once again, the hidden nature of illegal activities is an important obstacle in terms of one's ability to estimate them. Many estimates must rely on data on reported crimes, which account for only a fraction of the total criminal activities and serious crimes that occur in most statistically advanced countries. While authors adopting WGM invariably mention these issues and underline the recent improvement in the availability of criminal statistics, they generally pay scarce attention to the calculi and details underpinning their actual estimates of the proceeds of crime. At the same time, commentators note that, especially in terms of the first versions of the model, several of the necessary assumptions proposed by Walker rely either on his own experience or, apparently, a process of trial and error (Fontana, 2010; Unger & Busuioc, 2007). Consequently, the combination of unreliable data, dubious assumptions, and the lack of verification against alternative estimates of illicit market dimensions limit the capability of WGM accurately estimating the size of ML and IFFs (Fontana, 2010; Reuter, 2013).

Putting to one side the limitations pertaining to the quality of the data, data treatment, and adopted assumptions, a further conceptual issue undermines the effectiveness of adapting WGM to convincingly estimate IFFs. This pertains to the fact that IFFs do not concern merely cross-national forms of ML; rather, they also include tax abuses, terrorism financing, and the movement of capital related to the selling/purchasing of illicit goods and services in transnational crimes. The latter is an especially relevant component of the transnational dimension of criminal industries that the WGM is attempting to estimate. While the retail phase generates the largest part of revenues in many illicit industries, only a fraction of it turns into IFFs (Kilmer & Reuter, 2009; Reuter, 2013). In contrast, the international purchase of drug loads and containers of cigarettes and firearm shipments all move large amounts of illicit money that must be taken into consideration in estimates of IFFs, but are ignored by the *Walker Gravity Model* because they are not related to ML practices (Table 2.1).

Table 2.1 Summary of IFF estimation strategies

Method	Subgroup	Related illicit capital sources/predicate offenses	Main exploited data
Capital account-based estimates	Hot money narrow	Multiple combined; mainly corruption	Anomalies in the balance of payment (BoP)
	World Bank residual	Multiple combined; mainly corruption	Purposefully calculated anomalies in the BoP
Trade-based estimates	Mispricing	Multiple combined; mainly tax abuses	Import and export trade data at transaction or at national level
	Misinvoicing	Multiple combined; mainly tax and tariff abuses	
Combined capital account and trade approaches		Multiple combined; mainly tax evasion, bribery, and corruption	BoP and trade data
Offshore wealth estimates		Multiple combined	International asset and liability positions
Suspicious or unusual transaction analyses		ML; multiple predicate offenses; mainly terrorism financing and tax evasion	Transactions signaled by FIUs
Walker Gravity Model		ML; multiple predicate offenses; mainly drug trafficking	Crime and macroeconomic statistics

Source: author's elaboration
Note: the economics of IFFs is at an embryonic stage of development; available methodologies currently originate from different fields of research. This heterogeneity is reflected in the different perspectives through which researchers are trying to estimate IFFs, in the different types of IFFs that are considered, and the data that is exploited in the process

2.4 The Shared Limitations of the Available Methods

There is currently no single method capable of producing sound, clear, and incontestable figures of IFFs; rather, all the models outlined above are weakened by a range of potential biases or key information gaps (see Table 2.2) (Nitsch, 2016; UNODC, 2011). The remainder of this section outlines the common limitations of the available methods used in extant literature. The proposed analysis should help to better interpret the results of the various estimates based on these methods, not to mention aiding our understanding of the gap between current definitions of operationalization of IFFs and guiding the design of new estimation techniques.

2.4.1 The Proposed Methods Suffer Intrinsic Statistical Weakness

All the models outlined above rely on data and statistics – mainly economic and criminal ones – whose weaknesses may lead to biases in estimates. Given that the limitations in data collection and statistical reporting are often pronounced,

Table 2.2 Schematization of strengths/weaknesses of the available methodologies

	Strength and weaknesses							
	1	2	3	4	5	6	7	8
Capital account-based estimates	N	Y	P	P	N	Y	N	N
Trade-based estimates	N	Y	P	P	Y	Y	N	N
Combined capital-account and trade approaches	N	Y	P	P	P	Y	N	N
Offshore wealth estimates	N	N	P	P	P	Y	N	N
Suspicious or unusual transactions analyses	N	N	P	P	Y	N	N	P
Walker Gravity Model	N	P	P	P	N	Y	N	Y
	Legend:		YES		PARTIALLY		NO	

Source: author's elaboration

Note: the table provides a simplified classification of the respective methods based on their main strength/weaknesses. The numbers in the first line refer to the following parameters:

1. ROBOUST – the method relies on sound data/statistical bases
2. FEASIBLE – it is possible to produce estimates for a large number of countries in the world
3. ASSESSABLE – it is possible to assess the assumptions the method relies on and to evaluate their impact on the estimates
4. COMPARABLE – the method produces cross-nationally and longitudinally comparable estimates
5. TRANSFER RELATED – the estimates produced by the methods come together with information on the specific channel of transfer of the IFF
6. DOUBLE COUNTING FREE – the method is not undermined by major double-counting issues
7. CAPACITY – the method covers all types and channels of IFFs
8. SPECIFIC – the methods produce estimates that are attributable to specific sources of illicit funds and/or predicate offenses

especially in developing countries, similarly, biases in the estimate of IFFs will also be pronounced (Fontana, 2010). As noted by Cobham and Janský (2017a), improved methodologies can mitigate these effects up to a point, and, indeed, many of the surveyed approaches allow for producing estimates of the magnitude of IFFs in which we can have a degree of confidence. However, the inherent weaknesses of the available data mean that even sounder estimates might not necessarily lead to the development of indicators that are applicable for a global policy framework, such as the SDGs proposed by the United Nations. Indeed, there are a host of other problems shared by the proposed methods that stem from this unavailability of reliable data.

2.4.2 The Proposed Methods Rely on Assumptions Whose Relevance Is Difficult to Assess

As with any other form of estimation in the social sciences, researchers and analysts rely on assumptions in order to overcome the impossibility of collecting all of the relevant information to estimate IFFs (Spanjers & Salomon, 2017). According to authors as Nitsch (2012) and Forstater (2018), when adopting *trade-based approaches*, the magnitude and the relevance of these assumptions is such that the effectiveness of *trade mispricing as a method* through which to estimate IFFs is in itself questionable. While under-invoicing exports and over-invoicing imports may indeed be related to criminal behaviors, such as smuggling or carousel fraud, nonetheless, companies have dozens of reasons for over- and under-invoicing their trade activities; this could include over-invoicing exports to benefit from export subsidies and under-invoicing imports to avoid payment of import tariffs, which may offset each other (Nitsch, 2012). More generally, it is challenging to make assumptions about the global nature of industrial production; for example, it is common for companies to combine parts of products coming from different countries. This fact alone highlights how arduous it is to establish the precise origin of goods and determine where taxes should be paid, which, in turn, shows the limitations of using this information to estimate IFFs (Fontana, 2010; Spanjers & Salomon, 2017).

The role of assumptions is also crucial when performing capital account-based estimates, suspicious transaction analyses, and WGM, as discussed in the above presentation of these models. Simply put, measures of IFFs based on HMN and WBR include both legitimate and illegitimate capital transfers. With respect to HMN and WBR, inward and outward capital transfers of equal magnitude neutralize each other and lead to a null estimate of IFFs. As for *trade-based estimates*, measurement errors are indistinguishable from actual IFFs. *Suspicious transaction analyses* rely on a fundamental assumption, that is, those signals of suspicious transactions can be used as proxies of IFFs; the validity of such an assumption is questionable at best. The principal assumptions of the WGM concern several aspects of illicit markets of which it must estimate both the proceeds and the share of these proceeds that are laundered abroad (Reuter, 2013).

2.4.3 The Proposed Methods Do Not Produce Reliable Cross-National and Longitudinal Comparisons

The results produced by all these surveyed methods present manifold problems with respect to comparability, since the extent of the weaknesses in the data and accounting errors varies across countries and across time. These operational issues soon add up when one considers the fact that legal and normative acceptance of behaviors changes across time and space. Different jurisdictions have different definitions of IFF predicate offenses and, moreover, may differently label what constitutes dubious financial flows, which makes it hard to compare national estimates overall, as well as in relation to specific crimes (UNODC, 2011).

The problem of comparability is particularly severe with respect to *capital account* and *trade-based* estimates; data on intrafirm trades, on which the estimates of misinvoicing rely, have different standards from country to country. As Cobham and Janský (2017a, 13) observe: "[i]t is a question, when such research could be carried out at comparable cross-country basis with substantial worldwide coverage, but it is obviously not yet." When using the *suspicious transaction* method, it is crucial to consider that there is considerable variation between countries regarding reporting requirements, particularly related to the thresholds that may trigger a report, or the extent of non-monetary payment instructions (Unger & van Waarden, 2009; UNODC, 2011). Having said this, the effort required to collect this information is noteworthy. The *Walker Gravity Model* is similarly not exempt from this limitation. Indeed, there is vast criminological literature which discusses how different legal frameworks, the population's willingness to report illicit activities, law enforcement capacity, and accuracy of reporting offices impact upon cross-national criminal studies.

2.4.4 None of the Proposed Methods Account for All Possible IFFs

While international institutions and the public advocate for countermeasures are capable of addressing all components of IFFs – corruption-, criminal-, and tax-related capital – none of the aforementioned approaches are capable of measuring all these types of IFFs (GFI, 2018). In particular, models that rely solely on national accounts consider only part of the flows resulting from illicit activities, since profits stemming from contraband and corruption racketeering are not captured by these official statistics (Cobham & Janský, 2017a; Fontana, 2010). Moreover, none of the available data sources adequately reveal cash transactions across borders, same-invoice faking, misinvoicing services and intangibles, and hawala transactions, particularly those used in criminal pursuits (GFI, 2018). The impossibility of detecting these flows leads to the estimates that are produced by the presented methods being conservative in nature. This issue is exacerbated in cross-national and cross-crime comparisons, since the use of these instruments varies among crimes and between countries.

The available bottom-up approaches do not permit truly comprehensive estimates for three main reasons. Firstly, the WGM fails to take into account IFFs that are not related to ML. While considering only ML might not be problematic for crimes which do not necessarily lend themselves to international monetary flows, such as extortion or theft, the exclusive focus on ML is a severe limitation in the case of transnational traffics, in which a network of multiple transactions of goods/services connect many countries. Secondly, any method that aims to estimate IFFs by calculating the movements of different illicit proceeds requires developing new specific methodologies to estimate IFFs for every form of crime. Estimates have been produced with different degrees of reliability for illicit drug markets, counterfeiting, cigarette smuggling, and organized property crimes. On the contrary, it remains extremely difficult – perhaps impossible – to produce any meaningful estimates for serious crimes, such as human trafficking, waste trafficking, trafficking in firearms, extortion racketeering, usury, illegal gambling, and corruption (Reuter, 2013; Savona & Riccardi, 2015). The rationale behind the absence of such estimates has much to do with the severe lack of reliable data. Thirdly, models starting out from the proceeds of crime risk overlooking those financial flows which are illicit purely because of their transfer phase. Therefore, the WGM cannot be reliably adapted to estimate IFFs related to certain tax evasion schemes, in which the illicit capital is generated through the application of an illicit transfer scheme.

2.4.5 *Most Proposed Methods Do Not Produce Crime-Specific Estimates*

For advocacy purposes, it might be convenient to aggregate all possible forms of IFFs, and it might be acceptable to produce black box estimates. Nonetheless, for the purposes of policy and research, it would be more appropriate to produce estimates of IFFs that it is possible to disaggregate by the sources and methods used to move funds internationally, as crime-specific policies that differentiate between different illegal phenomena are more likely to be effective (Reuter, 2017). While none of the available methodologies are capable of capturing all forms of IFFs, most of them – especially top-down approaches – are limited by the fact that they give prominence to aggregated values and are unable to separate IFFs connected to different illegitimate activities.

Estimates that focus on anomalies and specific money-transferring channels inevitably combine different IFF types to some degree. Therefore, reliable estimates of individual IFF types capable of distinguishing between the movements of proceeds generated from drug trafficking from those linked to corruption cases or tax evasion may be difficult to obtain through these methods. The results of *trade-based estimates* are often intended to represent both fraudulent trade misinvoicing and strategic transfer pricing. While the former may as its express aim the moving of capital related to smuggling, tax and tariff evasion, paying bribes, and evading capital controls, the latter are often utilized by multinational companies for profit shifting (Forstater, 2018). By starting out from estimating the proceeds of crimes, the WGM thus performs better than other methods within this perspective. At the same time, the WGM does not allow for reconceiving of the generation phase of IFFs with any specific channel of transfer, which poses other problems for designing policies.

2.5 Conclusion

Direct measures of IFFs are hitherto not available, and it is perhaps unsurprising that the methods currently proposed in the literature are riven with manifold limitations. Present limitations, both in terms of our understanding and our capacity to define IFFs, inevitably impact upon the statistical operationalization of IFFs; in many cases, the relationship between the underlying conceptualization of IFFs and their empirical estimates remains obscure to say the least. The term IFFs is currently used to designate a vast universe of practices related to different crimes, concerned with different modi operandi, which poses multiple problems when it comes to producing figures.

The estimation methods that predominate in extant literature, especially top-down approaches, struggle to separate out the different constituent sources that flow into IFFs and do not allow for comparative assessments of the related predicate offenses and undesired behavior. Despite the fact that some of the methods are deemed adaptable enough to provide overall estimates of IFFs, in reality, they were often conceived for less ambitious purposes and, as such, begin to show their limitations when used for alternative, and more challenging, ends. Things are altogether more complicated when it comes to measuring IFFs that concern both flows of money directly connected to illegitimate activities and the laundering of the proceeds of crime. The consequences of this for designing countering policies and for research advancement are serious.

Each type of IFFs can exploit multiple transfer channels and each channel can facilitate multiple types of IFFs; the relationship between different IFFs and transfer methods varies over time and across countries. The available estimation procedures are limited in their ability to disentangle these complex relationships, and, hence, it is currently impossible to understand, simultaneously, where illicit money comes from, where they go, and how they move. These problems do not rise strictly from problematic conceptualizations of IFFs. By their nature, IFFs are hidden or disguised; in the same vein, the predicate offenses behind them are hidden or disguised. Henceforth, even if one develops a rigorous definition of IFFs, there remains a major issue concerning the statistical feasibility of measuring IFFs.

The contemporary relevance of IFFs in the international arena necessitates that we find a way to overcome these limitations, rather than abdicating oneself from the effort required to develop estimations. Two key considerations emerge from the analysis of the methods presented in this chapter. Firstly, new methods should clearly state which types of IFFs they are suitable for measuring: What are the sources of the funds related to the investigated IFFs? What are the predicate offenses related to these IFFs? In what specific sense are these actions illicit? In what manner this precise meaning of illicit is operationalized in the estimation procedure? In all probability, increasing the specificity in this way will result in a reduction of the "maximum capacity" of the estimates. Secondly, emergent approaches should be fully transparent, in the sense that they should outline all the underlying assumptions and the rationale behind the methodological choices. Indeed, this is the only way in which other researchers can reliably evaluate the strengths and weaknesses and, most importantly, assess the validity of their results.

Moving on from these considerations, the next chapter introduces an original approach for estimating IFFs related to the transnational trafficking of illicit goods. Subsequently, the fourth chapter delineates the underlying assumptions and calculi of the approach, for the express purpose of evaluating the relevance of these aspects for the overall reliability of the estimates.

References

Alstadsæter, A., Johannesen, N., & Zucman, G. (2017). Who owns the wealth in tax havens? Macro evidence and implications for global inequality. Working paper 23805. National Bureau of Economic Research.

Bhagwati, J. N. (1964). On the underinvoicing of imports. *Bulletin of the Oxford University Institute of Economics & Statistics, 27*(4), 389–397.

Blöker, K. (2003). Reporting suspicions of money laundering and whistleblowing under German law. *Journal of Money Laundering Control, 6*(1), 52–56.

Cobham, A., & Janský, P. (2017a). Illicit financial flows: An overview. UNCTAD. http://unctad.org/meetings/en/SessionalDocuments/tdb_efd1_bp_CJ_en.pdf

Cobham, A., & Janský, P. (2017b). 'Measuring misalignment: The location of US multinationals' economic activity versus the location of their profits. *Development Policy Review, 48*, 1–48.

Dalla Pellegrina, L., & Masciandaro, D. (2009). The risk-based approach in the new European anti-money laundering legislation: A law and economics view. *Review of Law & Economics, 5*(2), 931–952.

de Boyrie, M. E., Pak, S. J., & Zdanowicz, J. S. (2005a). Estimating the magnitude of capital flight due to abnormal pricing in international trade: The Russia–USA case. *Accounting Forum, Tax Avoidance and Global Development, 29*(3), 249–270.

de Boyrie, M. E., Pak, S. J., & Zdanowicz, J. S. (2005b). The impact of Switzerland's money laundering law on capital flows through abnormal pricing in international trade. *Applied Financial Economics, 15*(4), 217–230.

Eden, L. (2012). Transfer price manipulation. In P. H. Reuter (Ed.), *Draining development? Controlling flows of illicit funds from developing countries* (pp. 205–233). Washington, DC: The World Bank http://documents.worldbank.org/curated/en/305601468178737192/Draining-development-Controlling-flows-of-illicit-funds-from-developing-countries

FATF. (2010). *Money laundering using new payment methods*. Paris: Financial Action Task Force (FATF) http://www.fatf-gafi.org/media/fatf/documents/reports/ML%20using%20New%20Payment%20Methods.pdf

FINTRAC. (2017). *Guideline 2: Suspicious transactions*. Ottawa: Financial Transactions and Reports Analysis Centre of Canada (FINTRAC) http://www.fintrac.gc.ca/guidance-directives/transaction-operation/Guide2/2-eng.asp

Fontana, A. (2010). What does not get measured, does not get done'. The methods and limitations of measuring illicit financial flows. In *U4 brief* (Vol. 2). Bergen: U4 Anti-Corruption Resource Centre https://www.cmi.no/publications/file/3720-what-does-not-get-measured-does-not-get-done.pdf

Forstater, M. (2018). Illicit financial flows, trade Misinvoicing, and multinational tax avoidance: The same or different? In *CGD policy paper* (Vol. 123). Washington, DC: Center for Global Development https://www.cgdev.org/publication/illicit-financial-flows-trade-misinvoicing-and-multinational-tax-avoidance

Fuest, C., & Riedel, N. (2012). Tax evasion and tax avoidance: The role of international profit shifting. In P. H. Reuter (Ed.), *Draining development? Controlling flows of illicit funds from developing countries* (pp. 109–141). Washington, DC: The World Bank http://documents.worldbank.org/curated/en/305601468178737192/Draining-development-Controlling-flows-of-illicit-funds-from-developing-countries

GFI. (2018). *'Illicit financial flows' analytical methodologies utilized by global financial integrity*. Washington, DC: Global Financial Integrity http://www.gfintegrity.org/wp-content/uploads/2014/09/GFI-Analytics.pdf

Henry, J. S. (2012). *The price of offshore revisited*. Tax Justice Network. https://www.taxjustice.net/cms/upload/pdf/Price_of_Offshore_Revisited_120722.pdf

Hong, K. P., & Pak, S. J. (2017). Estimating trade misinvoicing from bilateral trade statistics: The devil is in the details. *The International Trade Journal, 31*(1), 3–28.

Johannesen, N., & Pirttilä, J. (2016). Capital flight and development: An overview of concepts, methods, and data sources. In *WIDER working paper series* (Vol. 095). World Institute for Development Economic Research (UNU-WIDER). https://ideas.repec.org/p/unu/wpaper/wp2016-95.html

Kar, D., & Cartwright-Smith, D. (2008). *Illicit financial flows from developing countries: 2002-2006*. Washington, DC: Global Financial Integrity. http://www.gfintegrity.org/storage/gfip/executive%20-%20final%20version%201-5-09.pdf

Kar, D., Cartwright-Smith, D., & Hollingshead, A. (2010). The absorption of illicit financial flows from developing countries: 2002-2006. In *SSRN scholarly paper ID 2335028*. Rochester, NY: Social Science Research Network. https://papers.ssrn.com/abstract=2335028

Kar, D., & Spanjers, J. (2015). *Illicit financial flows from developing countries: 2004-2013*. Washington, DC: Global Financial Integrity. http://www.gfintegrity.org/report/illicit-financial-flows-from-developing-countries-2004-2013/

Kilmer, B., & Reuter, P. H. (2009). Prime numbers: Doped, 2009, Online edition. https://foreignpolicy.com/2009/10/16/prime-numbers-doped/

Lensink, R., Hermes, N., & Murinde, V. (2000). Capital flight and political risk. *Journal of International Money and Finance, 19*(1), 73–92.

Nicolaou-Manias, K., & Wu, Y. (2016). Illicit financial flows estimating trade mispricing and trade-based money laundering for five African countries. GEG Africa discussion paper. Global Economic Governance. http://www.gegafrica.org/publications/illicit-financial-flows-estimating-trade-mispricing-and-trade-based-money-laundering-for-five-african-countries

Nitsch, V. (2016). Trillion dollar estimate: Illicit financial flows from developing countries. Working paper 227. Darmstadt discussion papers in economics. https://www.econstor.eu/handle/10419/141281

Nitsch, V. (2012). Trade mispricing and illicit flows. In P. H. Reuter (Ed.), *Draining development? Controlling flows of illicit funds from developing countries* (pp. 309–334). Washington, DC: The World Bank http://documents.worldbank.org/curated/en/305601468178737192/Draining-development-Controlling-flows-of-illicit-funds-from-developing-countries

Pak, S. J. (2012). *Lost billions transfer pricing in the extractive industries*. Norway: Publish What You Pay http://www.policyforum-tz.org/lost-billions-transfer-pricing-extractive-industries

Reuter, P. H. (2013). Are estimates of the volume of money laundering either feasible or useful? In B. Unger & D. van der Linde (Eds.), *Research handbook on money laundering* (pp. 224–232). Cheltenham, UK: Edward Elgar Publishing.

Reuter, P. H. (2017). *Illicit financial flows and governance: The importance of disaggregation*. Washington, DC: World Bank http://pubdocs.worldbank.org/en/677011485539750208/WDR17-BP-Illicit-Financial-Flows.pdf

Savona, E. U., & Riccardi, M. (2015). *From illegal markets to legitimate businesses: The portfolio of organised crime in Europe*. Trento: Transcrime – Università degli Studi di Trento http://www.transcrime.it/pubblicazioni/the-portfolio-of-organised-crime-in-europe/

Spanjers, J. (2015). *The methodology behind illicit financial flows from developing countries: 2004-2013*. Washington, DC: Global Financial Integrity. http://www.gfintegrity.org/the-methodology-behind-illicit-financial-flows-from-developing-countries-2004-2013/

Spanjers, J., & Salomon, M. (2017). *Illicit financial flows to and from developing countries: 2005-2014*. Washington, DC: Global Financial Integrity. http://www.gfintegrity.org/wp-content/uploads/2017/05/GFI-IFF-Report-2017_final.pdf

UNDP. (2011). *Illicit financial flows from the least developed countries: 1990-2008*. New York: United Nations Development Programme. http://content-ext.undp.org/aplaws_publications/3273649/IFFs_from_LDCs_web.pdf

Unger, B., & Busuioc, E. M. (2007). *The scale and impacts of money laundering*. Cheltenham, UK: Edward Elgar Publishing.

Unger, B., & van Waarden, F. (2009). How to dodge drowning in data? Rule- and risk-based anti money laundering policies compared. *Review of Law & Economics, 5*(2), 953–985.

UNODC. (2011). Estimating illicit financial flows resulting from drug trafficking and other transnational organized crimes. Research Report. In *Report*. Vienna: United Nations Office on Drugs and Crime http://www.drugsandalcohol.ie/16151/

Walker, J. (1995). *Estimates of the extent of money laundering in and through Australia*. Queanbeyan, NSW: John Walker Consulting, Prepared for AUSTRAC.

Walker, J. (1999). How big is global money laundering? *Journal of Money Laundering Control, 3*(1), 25–37.

Walker, J. (2007). *The extent of money laundering in and through Australia in 2004*. Melbourne: RMIT University http://www.criminologyresearchcouncil.gov.au/reports/200304-33.pdf

Walker, J., & Unger, B. (2009). Measuring global money laundering: 'The Walker gravity model. *Review of Law & Economics, 5*(2), 821–853.

Walker, J., & Unger, B. (2013). Measuring global money laundering: The 'Walker gravity model. In B. Unger & D. van der Linde (Eds.), *Research handbook on money laundering* (pp. 159–171). Cheltenham, UK: Edward Elgar Publishing.

Zucman, G. (2013). The missing wealth of nations: Are Europe and the U.S. net debtors or net creditors? *The Quarterly Journal of Economics, 128*(3), 1321–1364.

Chapter 3
A New Strategy to Estimate the Illicit Financial Flows

3.1 Introduction

In the previous chapters, I argued that there is not yet a consensus on how to define illicit financial flows (IFFs) and consequently on how to estimate them. The distinct natures of IFFs types, of their respective origins, and of their related channels of transfer require the adoption of specific measurement approaches for each of them. Accordingly, I here introduce a statistical methodology with which to estimate a specific form of IFF characterized by an illegitimate generation phase, rejecting the idea of designing a method able to take account of every form of IFF. The proposed *flow network approach* (FNA) focuses on the IFFs corresponding to the international payments directly related to the physical trafficking of illicit goods – eventually also services – between countries. These flows constitute an important component of IFFs related to many criminal markets and transnational crimes. At the same time, the proposed methodology provides an estimate of the gross value added (GVA) related to illicit industries. GVA constitutes the first step in estimating the amount of illicit money available for laundering overseas.

For illustrative purposes, the described FNA refers to the cocaine industry only. The focus on cocaine trafficking is primarily driven by the fact that the assumption formulation and calculations behind the estimate require quite detailed information, which – for the time being – is not readily available for many others transnational criminal activities (Reuter 2013; UNODC 2011). Moreover, the focus on cocaine allows for more direct appraisal of the crucial features of the proposed method as previous bottom-up attempts to estimate the IFFs focused on the cocaine industry (e.g., UNODC 2011). With all the caution that a possible adjustment to different crimes may require, the FNA is potentially extendable to other transnational illicit markets. IFFs deriving from corruption and theft/extortion-related crimes, which do not have an intrinsic transnational nature, would require, instead, the development of distinct methodologies.

A. Aziani, *Illicit Financial Flows*, SpringerBriefs in Criminology,
https://doi.org/10.1007/978-3-030-01890-0_3

The methodology, together with its resulting estimates, is tentative. It has several limitations due to the scarcity of original data and which primarily concern the impossibility of extending the method to all possible forms of IFF and its inability to provide information on the transfer methods adopted. Nevertheless, the FNA enables progress in the production of bottom-up estimates of the IFFs. It generates an estimate of IFFs directly related to transnational trafficking of illicit goods, and by detailing assumptions and calculi, it introduces advances in the estimation of the proceeds of crime functional to measuring IFFs related to international ML. Second, it may be a useful tool with which to determine the distinctive characteristics of illicit markets. When applied to traffics for which a minimum amount of information is available, the FNA allows for cross-sectional and longitudinal estimates which can be exploited in macrolevel panel data analyses conducted to evaluate crime reduction policies, which are absent in the extant literature.

The chapter is structured as follows. The body of the chapter presents the rationale for the proposed estimation approach; each of its subsections takes one of the four steps of the proposed methodology as its focal point. The Conclusion explains why estimates of the economic dimension of illicit industries are per se useful and summarizes the strengths and weaknesses of the proposed approach. The next chapter describes in detail the calculi, the data sources, and the assumption which are necessary to produce estimates with the FNA.

3.2 The Flow Network Approach

Transnational trafficking comprises two forms of IFFs. The first category concerns the flows associated with the transnational purchase or sale of illicit goods and services; they are directly connected to the generation and/or use phases of IFFs (see Chap. 1) and correspond to transactions in the illicit real economy. These IFFs are payments due to the purchase of a good or a service functional to running an illicit business; outward IFFs are generated by imports, while inward IFFs occur when illicit goods are exported to another country. For instance, a Dutch heroin trafficker who pays for a drug load coming from Bulgaria generates one of these IFFs. The second category regards the IFFs associated with the overseas laundering of the illicit proceeds deriving from any activity related to the illicit trafficking. IFFs related to the laundering phase are untied from the physical movement of illicit goods or the provision of illicit services and are not compulsory for the commission of their predicate offense. Once the Bulgarian trafficker receives his payment, he can move it to a safe haven in Cyprus and then transfer part of the money to Switzerland, giving origin to a second and a third IFF. The two types of IFFs are conceptually different; nonetheless, they are connected, and their distinction is not always immediate as shown by Fig. 3.1. When it comes to estimating the IFFs, the detachment of money laundering-related IFFs from any material aspect generates a risk of double counting.

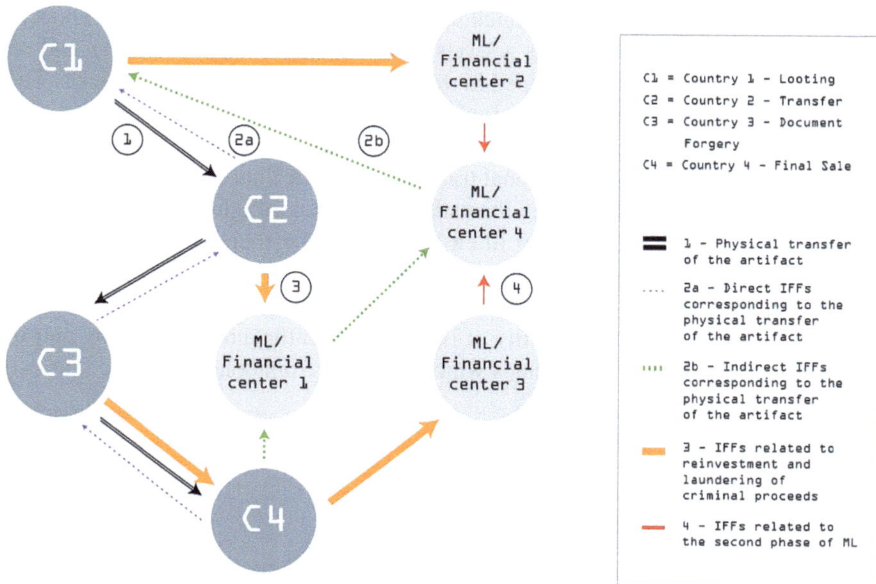

Fig. 3.1 One transnational crime, four kinds of IFFs; conceptual schematization of IFFs related to the illicit trade in antiquities.
(Note: the figure represents the potential IFFs connected to an archetypical illicit trade in antiquities. Scholars identify four recurring stages in the illicit antiquities trade. First, cultural artifacts are looted from cultural sites (step 1 in country 1); second, the artifacts are transported to different countries and they may change ownership (s2 in c2); third, it is necessary to falsify the documents to launder the artifacts before placing them on their final markets (s3 in c3); finally, the antiquities are sold to collectors as legitimate items (s4 in c4). Subjects with a specialized role operate in each of four stages and each stage ends with an economic transaction, which usually takes place at the international level and in different countries (Campbell 2013; Dietzler 2013). Since IFFs concern the transfer of money earned through illegal activities, each step of the illicit trade is likely to give origin to an IFF (i.e., 2a – blue-dotted lines) connected to the physical transaction of the artifacts in the real economy (i.e., 1 – double black lines). It is not mandatory that the financial transaction corresponding to the real-economy trade must follow the reverse path of the artifacts; the payment can transit to a third country or it may be saved there (i.e., 2b – green-dashed lines). Each of the actors involved in the transnational trafficking of the artifacts may give origin to a second stream of IFFs. The money that they have earned with the traffic of an artifact may be reinvested in further traffics or it may be internationally laundered, possibly in a country characterized by a low level of transparency of its financial institutions (i.e., 3 – large, full lines). Finally, each IFF related to money laundering activities may be further transferred to additional countries (i.e., 4 – thin, full lines). *Source: author's elaboration*)

I propose a tentative approach able to generate both longitudinal and cross-sectional estimates of the IFFs associated with the transnational purchase or sale of illicit goods and of the GVA related to transnational trafficking, dealing in roughly GDP-comparable terms. In turn, the IFFs associated with the transnational money laundering (ML) can be estimated starting from the overall GVA once we have a better understanding of criminal attitude toward ML and better data to measure it. The proceeds to be laundered abroad may be estimated by subtracting criminals' own consumes and money nationally laundered from the total estimate of the GVA.

The proposed approach is predicated upon both insights of scholars who conceptualize transnational trafficking as a series of physical and monetary flows and on data generation techniques developed in the field of criminal network analysis. The idea is to conceive transnational trafficking as a network of trading relationships among countries and national supply chains as a series of transactions that allow illicit goods to pass from international traffickers to their final users (see Fig. 3.2).

The methodology underpinning the estimate moves through four steps aimed at reconstructing the structure of the illicit trafficking and then to estimate its economic magnitude. The first step involves identifying the trafficking connections among countries. The second step consists of sizing each national market. The third step involves calculating the quantity of illicit goods trafficked between any pair of countries by combining the estimates which emerged from conducting the first two

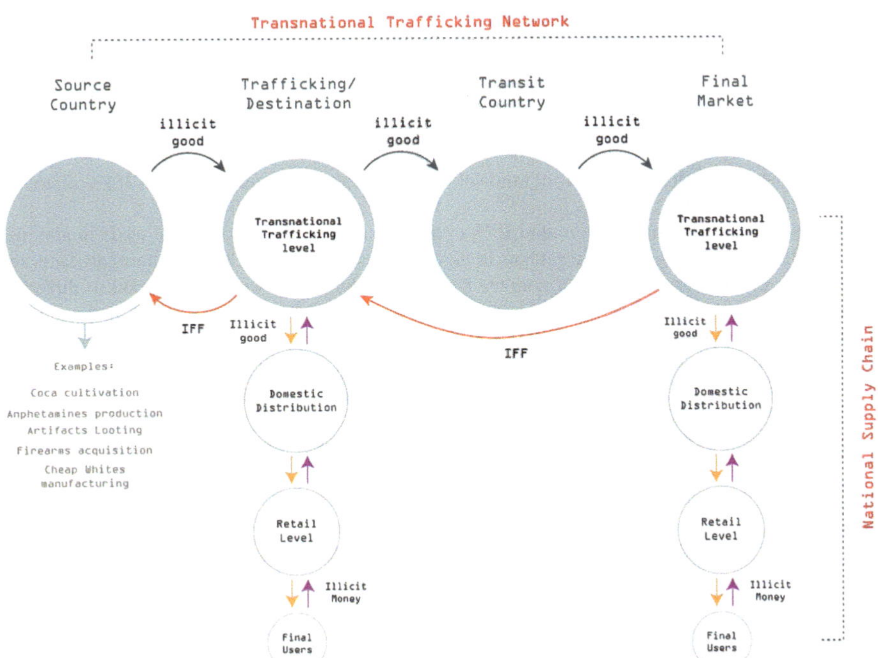

Fig. 3.2 Schematization of the flow network approach.
(Note: FNA consist of two main dimensions, the transnational network of countries involved in the illicit trafficking – horizontal dimension – and the national distribution chains, vertical dimension. The first dimension encompasses production countries, trafficking countries, transit countries, and final destination markets. As always, things are more complicated in reality. The same country can have different roles at the same time (e.g., hosting marijuana plantations, shipping marijuana to third countries, and importing from them other marijuana to be sold in the internal market). The second dimension is conceptualized in three main steps through which illicit goods reach their final users in exchange for money. Conceptualizing transnational trafficking in this way allows for estimating the GVA related to transnational and national illicit trafficking for each country along each route and at each step of the trafficking chain. *Source: author's elaboration*)

steps. Once the direction and size of international flows have been established, the fourth step reconstructs the organization of the supply chain in its different levels. Then it combines the weighted flows with prices and costs at different steps of the supply chain, which enables determination of the value added at national and international level, and estimation of the IFFs connected with physical shipments of illicit goods.

The value of transnational shipments of illicit goods corresponds to the inward and outward IFFs directly related to their transfer. The GVA generated by trafficking is the sum of the monetary value of the trafficking net of the costs of the goods sold; GVA denotes the revenues from the international trade, national distribution, and retail sale of the illicit goods, minus costs incurred through either purchasing the illicit goods that traffickers resell within the supply chain or losses due to interceptions by law enforcement agencies. The expression "gross value added" was originally proposed by Pedroni and Verdugo (2011), who defined GVA as the estimated tonnage of drug production multiplied by price per ton minus costs of intermediate input consumption.

Intermediate costs are not necessary for estimation of the IFFs corresponding to international shipments of illicit goods. Indeed, the considered IFF corresponds to the total flow overseas of money or other assets related to the shipments of illicit goods. In this perspective, it is not compulsory to disentangle the actual cost items that lead to that specific amount of money. In other words, the extent to which the monetary flow corresponds to traffickers' margin, direct costs, or expenses related to transport, protection, and document forgery is not relevant for the proposed estimate of the IFFs nor for the estimation of the GVA from which eventually to estimate ML-related IFFs.

Much like international traffickers, national distributors also incur other costs besides the mere purchase of illicit goods, such as transportation and protection (Paoli et al. 2009). Labor costs tend to be especially high because illegality forces the distribution system to operate in inefficient ways at retail, wholesale, and international levels. The constant risk of suffering losses to law enforcement agencies acts as a disincentive to invest in machinery and other instruments that could be confiscated from the traffickers. Although the proliferation of new communication technologies such as mobile phones and encrypted chatting services have transformed illicit dealing, in particular drug dealing, final distribution still requires far more personnel than what is required in a licit environment.

The proposed approach does not assume that all these costs are included in the margins of traffickers but does consider them to be a feature of the illicit economy of trafficking. Since the estimation of profits adopts a national perspective, it is not relevant which specific criminals earn this money as long as they are part of the trafficking business considered. In line with dominating interpretation of the term IFF, discussed in the Chap. 1, the estimate does not account for costs related to violence and conviction, which may be key components of costs within the trafficking industries, especially for cocaine (Reuter and Kleiman 1986; Reuter and Greenfield 2001).

3.2.1 Trafficking Routes from Source to Destination: Step 1

Transnational trafficking relates to the trade of goods that leave their source country and are then trafficked through an often large number of countries until they reach their final destination where they are consumed. Focusing on cocaine, the existence of organized drug flows between countries is a widely accepted notion among scholars; Paoli, Greenfield, and Reuter (2009) conceptualize transnational drug trafficking as a trade network and reveal that drug flows are relational in nature, and, as such, are ideally suited for the application of social network abstractions and analysis. Consequently, over the last decade, scholars have begun to use social network approaches to study national and transnational trafficking.

Conceiving international drug markets as a chain of economic exchange among countries may seem overly simplistic, but, in actual fact, the peculiar characteristics of drug trafficking actually confirm precisely the existence of these chains. All of the major illicit drugs including cocaine, illicit opiates, and amphetamine-type drugs are commodities whose commerce is necessarily international. The same holds true for trafficking in illicit firearms, wildlife, counterfeit and cheap white cigarettes, cultural artifacts, illegal timber, and many others. Indeed, while the origin of these illicit substances and goods tends to concentrate within a few specific areas, their consumption is often global. This is especially the case of cocaine.

Erythroxylum coca, the coca plant, is traditionally found in wet, tropical mountain forests and, more specifically, valleys with between 500 and 1500 meters elevation. Today, seven Latin American countries report some form of coca cultivation, but almost all coca cultivation is concentrated in specific valleys in Peru, Colombia, and Bolivia. What this means is that, except for cocaine, which is consumed in Andean countries, all remaining cocaine must cross at least one international border before it is consumed. The other aspect that makes most drug markets global is the relative ease of transportation. Cocaine is a compact good, and thus to ship it around the world is relatively straightforward from a logistical point of view (Caulkins 2015). Therefore, whenever cocaine is available in one country, it is likely to be soon available in other countries. These precise features of cocaine trafficking provide the rationale for conceptualizing it as a chain of transactions connecting drugs from producing countries to final consumers.

Historically, the lack of data has been a crucial factor hindering quantitative studies in the field of illicit trafficking. However, over the past decade, governments and international institutions have collected and issued a considerable amount of data concerning transnational trafficking, such as wholesale prices, seizures, and purity. Allied with a more mature understanding of the nature of transnational trafficking and with researchers' emergent capacity to analyze data in the form of a network, these datasets are an unprecedented source of information that scholars have begun to use to understand how illicit goods move across countries.

From an operational point of view, two main contributions to the modeling of drug trafficking as a network can be identified in the literature. The first stems from a series of studies by Boivin (2011, 2013, 2014), who used seizure cases and macrosocial network analysis to identify both the position of countries with respect to drug flows and understand the structural properties of heroin, cocaine, and cannabis trafficking networks. Chandra and colleagues developed the second main branch of research in the field of network analysis of drug trafficking flows, mainly by exploiting information on prices (Chandra and Barkell 2013; Chandra et al. 2011; Chandra and Joba 2015).

Boivin's principal contributions to the development of a drug trafficking network are the systematic use of information about seizures and the in-depth analysis of the limitations and pitfalls of such an approach. The construction of the network proposed in this book is deeply indebted to Boivin's (2011) work and thus shares, to a large extent, some of its limitations, which are discussed extensively in the description of each step of the estimation methodology proposed in the next chapter. Boivin (2011, 2013) constructed his drug trafficking networks using information on seizure cases collected from databases on significant drug seizures by the UNODC. Since these data provide only a partial picture of international drug trafficking network, Boivin integrated data on seizures with additional information. In particular, Boivin (2011, 2013) used anecdotal evidence reported by international organizations dealing with drug trafficking, such as the BINLEA, the EMCDDA, the INCB, and the UNODC, in order to complete the network.

Chandra and colleagues estimated the directions of transnational cocaine (Chandra et al. 2011) and heroin flows (Chandra and Barkell 2013) to European countries. To construct these networks, the authors analyzed and compared the wholesale prices of heroin and cocaine. Using anecdotal information collected from the *World Drug Report*, Chandra and colleagues identified "certain" drug flows (i.e., well-known drug trafficking connections whose relevance is recognized by law enforcement agencies and international organizations). They then assumed a link between any other pair of countries for which the drug price correlation exceeded a certain threshold constructed on the basis of the "certain" flows. By stating that the price of a drug increases with a new transaction, they were able to guess the directions of the flow, thus constructing directed binary networks of the international trafficking of heroin and cocaine (Chandra and Joba 2015).

Mapping the flows by looking at prices is an elegant maneuver which relies upon a solid theoretical basis: drug prices increase with the number of transactions from producing to destination countries (Caulkins 1995; Reuter 2014). However, the use of prices to weight the flows entails a complex assumption concerning the relationship between prices and volumes for which data are not currently available. Moreover, by working on single prices rather than ranges, Chandra and colleagues had to exclude any form of reciprocity in the relationships between countries within the drug trafficking network. While this is likely to be valid in most cases, it is not always so, as studies on drug seizures have documented and as Chandra and colleagues have themselves acknowledged (Chandra and Joba 2015). With respect to the construction of their trafficking network, Chandra and colleagues assumed the demand for cocaine to be inelastic with respect to price variations, thus ascribing changes in drug prices to shifts in its supply (Chandra et al. 2011). Most scholars argue the opposite: they posit that both cocaine trafficking and cocaine consumption are influenced by the price of the substance (Kleiman 1992; MacCoun et al. 2003). In light of these potential limitations, for the purposes of the proposed methodology, prices are utilized in order to check the meaningfulness of connections found through information on seizures, as opposed to identifying them.

3.2.1.1 The Proposed Modeling of the Transnational Trafficking Network

According to the strategy proposed here, the global cocaine trafficking network, as per the methodology proposed by Boivin (2011), is reconstructed using information from seizure cases reported by the UNODC individual drug seizure (IDS) databases. The availability of data on a specific route is adopted as a criterion for inclusion in the network. That is to say, the cocaine trade network includes all countries for which data are available, according to seizures which occurred in the period considered. The methodology proposed here expands upon previously adopted approaches by producing a network with minimal geographical boundaries, which does not draw upon anecdotal evidence and which may evolve in time. Since most trafficking routes are marked by constant changes, by modeling their evolution, it is possible to expand our knowledge of the trafficking phenomenon.

Information on seizures allows for the identification of pairs of countries exporting and importing cocaine with each other, as well as establishing the position of each country in the international trafficking network (Boivin 2011; UNODC 2015). At certain points, depending on the occurrence of the seizures, law enforcement agents are able to trace the movements of illicit shipments between countries. The transformation of available information into dyads (i.e., connections in the trafficking network) is straightforward, involving the origin, transit, and destination data being put into a relationship with the reporting countries, thus mapping the connection between those countries. By replicating the same procedure for all the countries, it is possible to map the entire network.

The reconstruction of the trafficking network may rely on information on seizure cases also for other transnational crimes, even if the data collection may be more challenging given the lack of comprehensive data repositories. For example, Savona and Mancuso (2017) conducted open source analyses to collect information on seizures and reconstruct the routes followed by illicit firearms. The same approach has been adopted to collect information on the transnational flows of illicit cigarettes targeting European countries (Transcrime 2015). In the field of human smuggling, transnational networks have been reconstructed by extracting information from police investigations (e.g., Campana 2018). Other information to model trafficking networks may come from the identification of forged documents or from information on the nationality of people detected while illegally crossing borders (Frontex 2018). By contrast, for example, Suvantola et al. (2017) have shown that no data are currently available to reconstruct the network of wastes trafficking reliably. Needless to say, the quality of the final estimate depends on the researcher's capacity to reconstruct the trafficking links: the weaker the underlying data and assumptions, the weaker the final estimate is.

3.2.2 *National Illicit Markets: Step 2*

The second step in estimating the IFF and the GVA generated by trafficking involves quantifying the amount of illicit goods consumed and seized in the countries considered in order to size their national markets. Quantifying the consumption of the illicit good considered is necessary to assess both the value of the market at retail level and the amounts moving along the illicit supply chain both transnationally and domestically. While the strategy is presented with reference to cocaine, researchers can apply similar approaches to the estimation of the volumes and values of shipments of heroin, illicit cigarettes, counterfeit products, and other illicit goods; the choice of the specific strategy for estimation of the consumption of the good concerned would depend on the specificities of the market considered and on available data.

There are still few studies estimating the economic dimension of drug markets, but the literature on sizing drug markets is more abundant, at least in developed countries. The series of studies promoted by the ONDCP's *What America's Users Spend on Illegal Drugs* (Kilmer et al. 2014; Rhodes and McDonald 1991) has improved, edition by edition, the methodology for sizing drug markets. Other rigorous studies which focus on the United States are those by Kilmer and Pacula (2009), Kilmer et al. (2011), and Kilmer et al. (2013a). As noted by Kilmer et al. (2014), outside the United States, scholars have principally focused on sizing illicit marijuana markets. However, non-American literature includes estimates for other illicit drugs, including cocaine. Authors and institutions have produced estimates of the scale of the market for cocaine in European countries (e.g., Kilmer, Taylor, et al. 2013b; Pudney et al. 2006). Examples of estimates of the size of cocaine markets outside the United States are also available for Australia (e.g., Ryan and Griffiths 2013) and Canada (e.g., Lippert and Walker 1997). The *World Drug Report* by the UNODC provides worldwide estimates of the size of illicit markets by macro regions. Other research adopts a multinational perspective, such as the studies by Kilmer and Pacula (2009) and UNODC (2015).

3.2.2.1 Methods to Size Drug Markets

The size of the national markets for drugs can be estimated by using information on the supply of or demand for drugs. Seizure-based and production-based estimates are the principal approaches on the supply side, whereas consumption-based and expenditure-based are the principal forms of demand-side estimates (Hickman and Taylor 2002; Kilmer et al. 2014).

Supply-Side Estimate

The most straightforward supply-side estimate is the seizure-based one. Seizure-based estimates multiply seizures by an estimated interception rate, which helps ascertain the mass of illicit goods available. While this approach is simple to implement and relies on readily available data (i.e., seizures data), it tends to provide unreliable estimates because there is no a priori information on interception rates. Seizures simultaneously reflect the dimension of the illicit flows, law enforcement resources and priorities, and the strategies adopted by criminals to avoid interdictions (Kilmer and Hoorens 2010). At present, it is ordinarily impossible to disentangle these three factors. Moreover, not all of the illicit goods available in a market are consumed locally; in many cases, a portion is exported to a third country. Therefore, to estimate the level of national consumption, it is also necessary to determine the masses of drug which are exported abroad (Reuter and Majmundar 2015). It is these limitations which have restricted the adoption of this method.

Production estimates are the principal supply-side approach to sizing cocaine and heroin markets. With respect to cocaine, production-based estimates begin with an evaluation of the soil used to grow coca; then, the potential production of cocaine is quantified considering yields per hectare, eradications, laboratory efficiency, and seizures. The acquisition and use of these data are undoubtedly complex, requiring corrections that take into account cloud cover, eradications, spraying, dates of acquisition, etc. The calculation of the effective production of coca leaves is perhaps even more complex than estimating the total area under cultivation. After estimating the total production, researchers use a series of conversion factors (e.g., dry weight per unit weight harvested, kilos of coca base per coca paste) to pass from masses of coca leaves to the potential production of cocaine. These steps also rely on a series of assumptions with respect to the techniques used to transform it, such as the precursors used, the kind of laboratory where the process takes place, the ability of the chemists, and so forth (Thoumi 2002; Kilmer et al. 2011). Seizures and other law enforcement interventions, which can reduce the amount of available coca derivatives, must also be included in this estimate.

After determining the total production in the source countries, the consumption of cocaine in any given country is estimated by making assumptions about the share of potential production that is successfully exported to that particular destination. These assumptions mainly concern the masses of seizures that occurred in prior stages of the supply chain, the level of consumption occurring in other markets, and the quantity of cocaine stockpiled in producing countries. A further factor to take into account is the time lag between harvesting the coca bush, cocaine processing, and trafficking. Cocaine produced in a given year may take up to a year or more to reach consumer markets (Ehleringer et al. 2012).

Difficulties regarding estimation of the area under coca cultivation, of the efficiency of all the chemical processes, and assumptions about the directions of drug flows characterize production-based estimates. These concerns, together with a long series of inconsistent reporting by governmental agencies and international organizations, have induced several authors to express skepticism about this method.

Demand-Side Estimates

Consumption-based models combine the prevalence of use with information on the typical number of days of consumption and the consumed amount per use-day, by user type, in order to estimate the total consumption of a given population. The main strength of these approaches is that, taking the destination country as a starting point, they permit the production of country-specific estimates wherever national data are available. The consumption-based approach is far from being perfect for a number of reasons that will be outlined in the following subsections. The expectation is that all the estimates produced with the proposed methodology will be replicated once better data on national cocaine markets become available.

3.2.2.2 The Proposed Modeling of the Size of the National Markets

Taking the mentioned limitations into consideration, the proposed methodology adopts a consumption-based approach, which is the most widely used demand-side estimate method and the only one which allows for reasonable country-specific estimates given the available data (T. P. Johnson 2014). The adoption of the demand-side approach leads to the assumption that the overall quantity of cocaine circulating within countries is equal to the overall quantity of cocaine consumed plus seizures. In turn, the amount of drug entering any specific country has to be equal to internal consumption, seizures, and exports to third countries. Losses and stockpiles are other components of the quantity of coca derivatives flowing from country to country (Ehleringer et al. 2012). Neither of these two elements is included in the estimate proposed by this methodology.

To assume that accidental losses are a trivial share of the total of the cocaine available in any market should not introduce any major bias into the estimate (Willis et al. 2010). The high value of cocaine induces every person taking part in its trafficking to pay especial attention when managing it. Some analysts suggest that traffickers may manage possible shortages in the supply of cocaine by stockpiling it (Mazzitelli 2011; Madeira et al. 2011). However, evidence about cocaine stockpiles is particularly scant in the literature (Ehleringer et al. 2012) and tends to indicate that stockpiles in consumer markets are negligible (Hughes et al. 2012). By assuming that stockpiles are in producing countries, where they are more likely to be, as opposed to elsewhere, it is possible to ignore them in the estimate of the value of the cocaine market for any given country.

3.2.3 The Dimension of the Shipments: Step 3

Both the branches of research developed by Boivin and by Chandra and colleagues model international trafficking as a binary network in which connections between countries can be present or absent, but do not have different magnitudes. Boivin and Chandra's networks provide information on whether or not two countries are connected by drug trafficking activities, as well as in which direction(s) the drug flow goes.

The reasoning behind these authors' decision to exclude the edge weights from their analysis of trade networks is twofold. Firstly, including information on the quantity of illicit goods traded between any two countries requires estimation of the size of illicit markets for each country. This exercise is challenging and forces researchers to accept particularly strong assumptions given the paucity of certain classes of fundamental data, especially when focusing on multiple countries (Kilmer et al. 2011, 2015). Secondly, in order to develop trafficking-weighted networks, it is necessary to weight the magnitude of each flow with respect to all the other flows targeting the same market. This second task also presents numerous difficulties and requires acceptance of rigid assumptions which limit the reliability of the estimate itself. However, trafficking networks are intrinsically weighted, so that ignoring the dimension of the flows results in a loss of fundamental information when it comes to estimating the IFFs.

The studies on the flows of opiates from Afghanistan to the Western Europe constitute a third methodological contribution, which introduced the dimension of the flows in the analysis (UNODC 2015; Berlusconi et al. 2017). This branch of studies proposed reflections that led directly to the development of the estimation approach proposed here. While the networks produced by previous research analyzed the presence or the absence of connections, UNODC's (2015) study expanded upon this reasoning by estimating volumes of drug shipments and monetary flows along the heroin supply chain of the extended Balkan route. Moving on from the opiate business model presented by the FATF/OECD/UNODC (2014), which identified production, manufacturing, distribution, and retail sale as the fundamental steps of the illicit industry in opiates, UNODC's (2015) study estimated the gross profit yielded from Afghan opium.

UNODC (2015) identified drug flows by studying seizure cases and anecdotal evidence from reports produced by international institutions. After identifying the network, it was necessary to weight the relevance of each connection within it. The UNODC (2015) estimated the volume of the flows by confronting the volume of opiates seized between two countries with the total volume of seizure at entrance performed by the importing country. The higher the seizures of illicit opiates coming from that specific origin, the higher the flow from there. Subsequent studies followed in the footsteps of these analyses in order to investigate the determinants of the geopolitical configuration of international trafficking of heroin (e.g., Berlusconi et al. 2017).

3.2.3.1 The Proposed Modeling of Size of the Shipments

Information on the mass of seizure cases – alternatively the number of seizures or of seized goods, depending on the traffic under analysis – permits estimation of the amount of the trafficking between two countries with respect to others. The basic rationale here is that the volumes of seizures may be indicators of the volumes of illicit flows. In its simplest form, the idea is that, considering any importing country, if seizures of illicit goods coming from a specific country are more abundant than seizures along another connection, then trafficking along the first connection is likely to be more copious than along the second.

In reality, factors other than the actual size of the flow influence this relationship; a particular route may be more successfully targeted by law enforcement, for example, or it may be that the data reporting systems of countries along the first route are comparatively more efficient than those of countries along the second route. It follows that it is preferable to estimate the relative weight of flows on a country-by-county basis. I propose to divide the amount of seizures intercepted while flowing between two countries by the total seizures referring to the importing country, thus obtaining an estimate of the relevance of that connection for that specific importing country. By replicating the procedure for every year, it then becomes possible to understand how the importance of different trafficking routes has evolved over time. It is then necessary to estimate the amount of illicit goods flowing along each connection as identified and weighted.

In the above-discussed study by Paoli, Greenfield, and Reuter (2009), the authors developed what they called a "global distribution model" to track opium flows. Their contention was that drugs produced must at some point either be consumed or seized. Therefore, starting from estimation of drug production in source countries, by subtracting seizures and consumptions country by country, it is possible to infer the amounts of drugs flowing along the international supply chain. The FNA applies the same general principle but instead relies upon demand-side estimates, which the literature considers more robust than supply-side ones with respect to several illicit markets; illicit goods that have been seized or consumed in a certain country must have been imported from somewhere, with countries that host their production being the obvious exception.

The proposed FNA assumes that each country imports a volume of illicit goods equal to the consumption, seizure, and exports of those goods. The inclusion of seizures in the estimate of imports is straightforward: the illicit goods seized in a certain country arrived in that country at a certain point in time. While it is simple to include seized volumes in the estimates of imports, the model lacks the capacity to adjust the levels of consumption according to variations in seizures. Even though authors such as Reuter and Kleiman (1986) assert, with respect to drugs, that the data indicate that dramatic increases in levels of enforcement have not affected the availability of drugs, consumption is likely to decrease as consequence of intense variation in interdiction rates. Other studies estimating the economic dimension of drug trafficking do not model this dynamic (e.g., Baldassarini and Sallusti 2014) (Fig. 3.3).

Whenever the reconstruction of the trafficking network under analysis includes almost all relevant countries, no further assumption is required to model imports from and exports to countries not included in the analysis. The demand for illicit goods in other countries allied with the structure of the network determines the mass of the flows transiting in a country, only to be later exported to a third one. Indeed, the model assumes that exports depend on the mass of cocaine consumed and seized in the next country in the trafficking network.

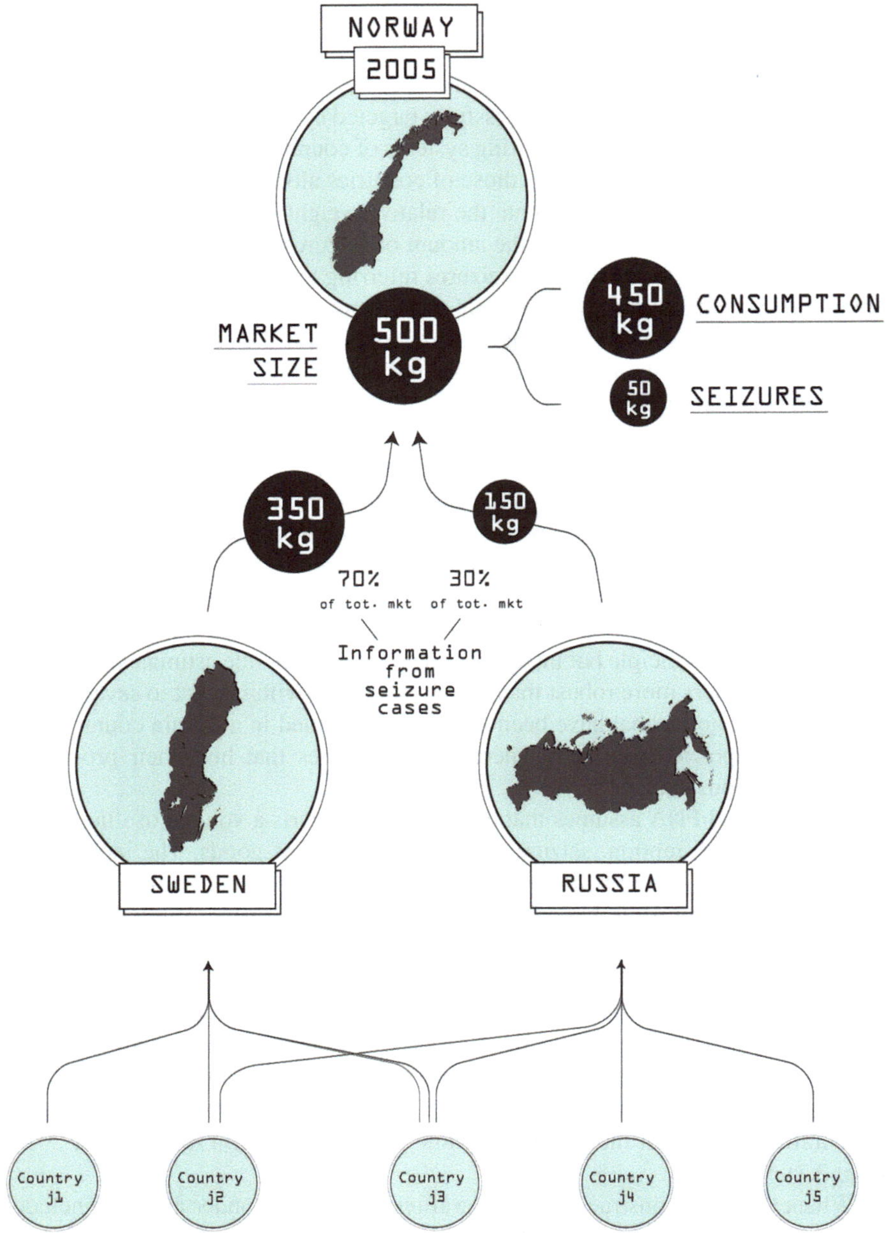

Fig. 3.3 A graphic representation of the sizing of the flows.
(Note: For example, the structure of the illicit network might show that Norway, in 2005, had no export connections and 70% of its imports – e.g., of cocaine – came from Sweden and 30% from Russia. At the same time, the estimate of the size of the market might indicate that, in the same year, the Norwegian market accounted for 500 kg of cocaine, of which about 10% were seizures. Then, by combining the two figures, it emerges that cocaine flows from Sweden to Norway and from Russia to Norway accounted, respectively, for 350 kg and 150 kg of cocaine in 2005. In turn, the model registers the information that through Sweden and Russia have to flow 350 kg and 150 kg of cocaine destined to Norway, in addition to the amount necessary to satisfy their national markets. The volumes flowing along each connection are estimated by the simultaneous combination of these calculi for all the countries in the network. *Source: author's elaboration*)

3.2.4 *The Supply Chain of Illicit Markets: Step 4*

The modeling of the supply chain depends on the specific illicit market under analysis, whose functioning at both the domestic and international level may have specificities related to the criminal *modi operandi*. Bearing in mind that the overall aim is estimation of the IFFs, this step of the methodology should help in subdividing overall GVA by categories of actors, assuming that different types of actors have different propensities to launder their proceeds overseas.

With respect to cocaine, while scholars agree on the existence of multiple stages in the supply chain of drugs between production and the final consumers, their number and their true nature are hotly debated (Caulkins et al. 2016). For instance, there is no clear consensus as to what constitutes upper-level drug trafficking. Terms used in the literature include "upper-level" and "higher-level drug traffickers," "importers," "smugglers," "distributors," "suppliers," "wholesalers," "drug brokers," "go-betweens," and "facilitators" (Desroches 2007). Much as there is no definitive definition of the different levels of the drug markets, so there is no overarching consensus as to how revenues should be divided among these levels (Desroches 2007; Moore et al. 2005; Bright et al. 2011).

It is known that most of the value added in the supply chain is accrued when drugs are distributed within consuming countries (Reuter and Kleiman 1986). On the contrary, farmers cultivating coca plants or opium poppies receive only a minuscule fraction of the final retail value of drugs. The most significant increases in value occur when the drug is smuggled across national borders. However, the largest absolute increase occurs within final importing markets. This is because at the end of the distribution chain, the risks per gram are greatest; most of the money in consumer markets flows to domestic distributors, only some of whom are foreign nationals (Reuter and Greenfield 2001). This knowledge base on the distribution of revenues within the supply chain should aid design of the model. However, it does not offer indications on how precisely to structure the supply chain because it explicates dynamics in terms of revenues rather than profits. Therefore, the current methodology schematizes the supply chain in such a way that it is not able precisely to represent the cocaine supply chain; the model instead guides the estimation of complex data, such as IFFs and GVA emerging from the trade of cocaine.

3.2.4.1 The Proposed Modeling of the Supply Chain

For estimation of the GVA and IFFs, I propose to divide the illicit supply chain into three main blocks or components: high/international level, intermediate distribution level, and retail level. This methodology uses the expression "high international level" to denote the trafficking of large loads of illicit goods across national borders, allied with high-level sales to national distributors. "Intermediate distribution level" refers to traffickers who purchase illicit goods from international traffickers and distribute them to local retailers without taking part in international transactions or interacting with consumers. Given the broad definition that other studies apply to high-level traffickers, the literature occasionally includes similar actors among high-level traffickers, labeling them as "wholesalers" or "distributors."

Dealers that purchase illicit goods from intermediate distributors and sell them to final consumers operate at the retail level. Just focusing on drug, also the term "drug dealer" has referred to a variety of figures and roles. According to Caulkins et al. (1999), for example, there are four distinct types of sellers, with systematic differences across types in the proportion of sales revenue retained. Nonetheless, this is the category of actors whose definition is the least controversial and upon which the vast majority of the literature is concentrated. Retail-level dealers constitute the majority of people taking part in drug trafficking, and they often engage in drug dealing to finance their own consumption (Tunnell 1993).

Finally, the amount of drug traded at each level is combined with corresponding prices to obtain the GVA at each level. The outward IFFs related to the transnational trafficking of cocaine, for each country, emerge as the product of the imported mass of cocaine multiplied by its estimated price. Conversely, inward IFFs related to the physical movement of cocaine correspond to the money received for the exports. The section *Estimating the Economic Value of Drug Trafficking* in the next chapter presents data, sources, and assumptions necessary to produce this specific estimate.

3.3 Conclusion

The proposed FNA constitutes an innovative approach to estimate the IFFs related to transnational trafficking. As by product of the estimation of the IFFs, the FNA allows for producing original estimates of the economic value (i.e., the gross value added) of trafficking industries and illicit markets. The next subsection explains why the use of new estimates to analyze the economic patterns of transnational crimes represents an original contribution of this book to the studies on serious transnational crimes. The rest of the conclusions discusses the principal limitations and advantages of the FNA for the estimation of IFFs.

3.3.1 Why Estimate the Economic Value of Transnational Trafficking Per Se?

The interest of criminologists in illicit markets is nothing new, of course. The study of illicit markets rather than criminal offenders has its origins in the classic studies conducted on the American organized crime syndicates during the prohibition era (Landesco 1932), not to mention studies on the emergence of black markets in Europe during World War II (Louwage 1951). This branch of research has grown greatly since the end of the 1960s, with the study of drug policies and drug markets (Cave and Reuter 1988), as well as of criminal enterprises (Schelling 1967), due in part to the growing contribution of economists to criminological literature. More recently, authors have argued that the understanding of issues related to illicit markets, like the systemic violence characterizing some of them, requires deeper comprehension of the underlying economic dynamics (Kleiman 2004; Ousey and Lee 2007).

Unfortunately, the illegality of drug trafficking, illicit waste management, cigarette trafficking, etc. makes it difficult to estimate their size and value (Reuter 2013; Savona and Riccardi 2015; Thoumi 2005). In particular, even though several studies are buttressed by sophisticated empirical methodologies, none of them has proved truly able to determine the scale of profits or the monetary value of illicit markets. Rather, authors have used proxies like estimates of production or shortages of supply, and most of the commonly cited figures refer to total revenues at a retail level or to indicative losses for the licit economy (Reuter and Greenfield 2001; Savona and Riccardi 2015). Consequently, they include neither earnings from international illicit trade nor any form of cost. Yet these alternative indicators (e.g., revenues, supply, seizures) are simply incapable of representing the full complexity of the economic dynamics of illicit markets, nor do they help in estimating the IFFs. Even in the less structured illicit industries, a multitude of factors may determine important variations in the value of the market, as well as the respective margins for traffickers. Arrests, seizures, increases in demand, modification of trafficking routes, spikes in the production of drugs or other illicit goods, and shifts in use toward other goods are only a few of the numerous factors that may cause variations in traffickers' profits. There are manifold potential simultaneous combinations of several of these factors, and their overall effect is usually complex to evaluate. Estimating the size of the market, in terms of both volume and expenditure, is critical for thorough understanding of the full impact of interventions intended to influence demand and/or supply.

The lack of economic estimates of illicit markets reverberates within the empirical analysis of their broader impacts on other societal issues. More rigorous information is crucial for developing theoretical analyses and implementing more effective counter-policies (Kleiman 2009). Understanding whether a market is expanding or contracting, if it is worth thousands, millions, or billions of dollars, or if it accounts for tens or hundreds of metric tons is integral to both expanding theoretical knowledge about the functioning of illicit markets and properly evaluating the impact of policies aiming at contrasting them.

In consideration of this, the proposed approach presents a series of strengths that relate to the contextual estimation of the GVA per se. The use of new estimates to analyze the economic patterns of transnational crimes directly instead of using proxies like retail or wholesale prices, volume or number of seizures, and prevalence of consumption/use is an important step forward in the study of serious transnational crimes. Moreover, with respect to different transnational crimes, while quantitative research had mainly focused on consumer countries, in particular the United States, the FNA promises to produce information for a much larger group of nations. Therefore, an approach focusing on the economic dimension of the phenomenon and on estimates based on FNAs should enhance our understanding of many aspects of illicit markets. More reliable data on illicit consumption and illicit physical flows would enable refinement of the estimates of profits put forward in this chapter.

In the same vein, the FNA adopted to estimate profits generated in the illicit markets also permits the production of original estimates on seizure rates calculated as the ratios between seizures occurring in a country and total illicit inflows. These data make it possible to go beyond the traditional limitations of using seizures as measures of law enforcement. Most studies usually rely on indicators which are not able to express the effectiveness of law enforcement interventions and therefore do not provide valid information about their impact on criminals (Miron 2001; Kleiman 2009; Kilmer et al. 2014).

3.3.2 Main Weaknesses of the Flow Network Approach

The above-outlined methodology is not without its limitations. They mainly concern three aspects and are shared with most of the alternative IFF estimation strategies presented in the literature (see Table 3.1). Primarily, the scarcity and scant reliability of original data lead to the adoption of strong assumptions and introduce weaknesses into the estimates themselves, as discussed in the next chapter.

Secondly, the proposed methodology is unable fully to address the complexity of IFFs even if it concentrates only on the IFFs related to the physical movement of illicit goods – alternatively on illicit service providing – among the many possible ones. By concentrating on the functioning of illicit industries, the FNA provides no support in assessing what are the transfer methods used to move the illicit funds overseas. Traffickers may purchase their drug loads using wire transfers, smuggling bags full of cash, or falsifying invoices. Estimating the value of illicit transnational transactions does not provide information on the exploited channels to transfer the illicit capital abroad. In addition, FNA does not allow tracing the certain direction of IFFs. The countries of departure, transit, or destination of illicit goods are not necessarily the countries where the corresponding inflows and outflows of money or assets used for the settlement take place. Monetary and cocaine flows may be partly disconnected; some of the actors operating in any country may not be citizens of that country nor of a country immediately connected to it in the trafficking network. These traffickers may repatriate part of their profits, thus generating a misalignment between drugs and monetary flows. ML techniques based on the exploitation of banking secrecy in financial havens is another dynamic which causes drug flows and monetary flows not to fully overlap.

At present, our knowledge about the propensity to save and consume by people involved in drug trafficking or other illicit markets is extremely limited. This applies both to members of organized criminal groups and to independent actors. Scholars hypothesize that people active in these illicit industries are more prone to consumption than people engaged in legal occupations because of a lower expected value of their future (Reuter 2017). Our understanding of these criminal behaviors is simply

Table 3.1 Schematization of strengths/weaknesses of the flow network approach

1. Robust	No
2. Feasible	Partially
3. Assessable	Partially
4. Comparable	Yes
5. Transfer-related	No
6. Double Counting Free	Yes
7. Capacity	No
8. Specific	Yes

Note: The table provides a simplified schematization of the strengths and weaknesses characterizing the FNA. As for the methods analyzed in the second chapter, the numbers and the labels in the first column refer to the following parameters:

1. Roboust – The method relies on sound data/statistical bases.
2. Feasible – It is possible to produce estimates for a large number of countries in the world.
3. Assessable – It is possible to assess the assumptions the method relies on and to evaluate their impact on the estimates.
4. Comparable – The method produces cross-nationally and longitudinally comparable estimates.
5. Transfer-related – The estimates produced by the methods come together with information on the specific channel of transfer of the IFF.
6. Double counting free – The method is not undermined by major double counting issues.
7. Capacity – The method covers all types and channels of IFFs.
8. Specific – The methods produce estimates that are attributable to specific sources of illicit funds and/or predicate offenses.

Source: author's elaboration

too weak for it to be possible to include these elements in any estimate of the IFFs. In the future, improved information and data on these aspects of illicit markets will make it possible to improve the quality of estimates.

Finally, distinct methodological approaches should be developed for the IFFs deriving from corruption, predatory crimes, and licit or legal activities. The FNA rotates around the modeling and reconstruction of the national and transnational trafficking networks. Clearly, the methodology is weak for licit and illicit activities for which this structure is meaningless. Most predatory crimes do not have any transnational dimension, and the *modus operandi* behind them does not foresee transnational movements of goods. Therefore, an approach like the one presented here, estimating the financial flows related to the international purchase and sale of illicit products, would be meaningless for analyzing these crimes.

3.3.3 Main Strengths of the Flow Network Approach

Together with these significant shortcomings, the proposed approach has a number of strengths. The association between the estimates and the underlying concept of IFFs is clear; FNA makes it possible to estimate the IFFs directly connected to real-economy illicit transactions. Other approaches, focusing on ML schemes or on aggregated statistics, ignore this class of IFFs or are not able to disentangle them from IFFs emerging from other illegitimate activities. The capability of addressing the IFFs related to these specific sources of illicit capitals is an important feature, given their importance for illicit markets and transnational crimes. By starting from the modeling of specific transnational crimes, the FNA approach makes it possible to compare different component sources of IFFs (e.g., cocaine trafficking vs. illegal wildlife trade) at country level. In turn, this feature aids understanding of the true nature of IFFs as well as in countering them and their predicate offenses. At the same time, the FNA does not rely on information related to the illicit transfer of capitals; therefore, estimates of the IFFs produced by adopting the FNA are free from any risk of double counting illicit capital movements.

The proposed estimate of the GVA is an advance on the estimates proposed as the first step of the *Walker Gravity Model*. In particular, it comes with the details necessary to evaluate its reliability and to modify it whenever more reliable data become available. The next chapter is centered on step-by-step illustration of the data, assumptions, methodologies, and calculi. Moreover, disaggregation of the proceeds along the supply chain will support the estimate of the amount of money that is actually more likely to be internationally laundered, once we will have a better understanding of criminals' attitude toward the use of their proceeds.

More in general, the FNA entirely relies on readily and publicly available data, which guarantee, with varying levels of reliability, the feasibility of the estimates at least for those traffics for which some data do exist (e.g., illicit opiates, illicit cigarettes, counterfeiting). In this regard, the estimate can potentially be constructed across time, across many jurisdictions, and regardless of the channels actually used to move the illicit funds. This specific benefit concerns not only estimation of the IFFs but more in general of the economic size of illicit markets, which are still particularly scant in the literature.

References

Baldassarini, A., & Sallusti, F. (2014). *Estimating illegal drug flows in Italy: A statistical approach.* Presented at the 8th ISSDP Conference, Rome.

Berlusconi, G., Aziani, A., & Giommoni, L. (2017). The determinants of heroin flows in Europe: A latent space approach. *Social Networks, Crime and Networks, 51*, 104–117.

Boivin, R. (2011). *Le monde à l'envers: analyse de la structure du trafic transnational de drogues illicites.* Montréal: Université de Montréal. https://papyrus.bib.umontreal.ca/xmlui/handle/1866/6068.

Boivin, R. (2013). Drug trafficking networks in the world-economy. In *Crime and networks.* London; New York: Routledge http://erdr.org/textes/boivin.pdf

Boivin, R. (2014). Risks, prices, and positions: A social network analysis of illegal drug trafficking in the world-economy. *The International Journal on Drug Policy, 25*(2), 235–243.

Bright, D. A., Hughes, C. E., & Chalmers, J. (2011). Illuminating dark networks: A social network analysis of an Australian drug trafficking syndicate. *Crime, Law and Social Change, 57*(2), 151–176.

Campana, P. (2018). Out of Africa: The organization of migrant smuggling across the mediterranean. *European Journal of Criminology, 15*, 481.

Campbell, P. B. (2013). The illicit antiquities trade as a transnational criminal network: Characterizing and anticipating trafficking of cultural heritage. *International Journal of Cultural Property, 20*(2), 113–153.
Caulkins, J. P. (1995). Domestic geographic variation in illicit drug prices. *Journal of Urban Economics, 37*(1), 38–56.
Caulkins, J. P. (2015). After the grand fracture: Scenarios for the collapse of the international drug control regime. *Journal of Drug Policy Analysis, 0*(0).
Caulkins, J. P., Johnson, B. D., Taylor, A., & Taylor, L. J. (1999). What drug dealers tell us about their costs of doing business. *Journal of Drug Issues, 29*(2), 323–340.
Caulkins, J. P., Disley, E., Tzvetkova, M., Pardal, M., Shah, H., & Zhang, X. (2016). Modeling the structure and operation of drug supply chains: The case of cocaine and heroin in Italy and Slovenia. *The International Journal on Drug Policy, 31*, 64–73.
Cave, J. A., & Reuter, P. H. (1988). *The interdictor's lot: A dynamic model of the market for drug smuggling services*. Santa Monica, CA: RAND Corporation.
Chandra, S., & Barkell, M. (2013). What the price data tell us about heroin flows across Europe. *International Journal of Comparative and Applied Criminal Justice, 37*(1), 1–13.
Chandra, S., & Joba, J. (2015). Transnational cocaine and heroin flow networks in Western Europe: A comparison. *International Journal of Drug Policy, 26*(8), 772–780.
Chandra, S., Barkell, M., & Steffen, K. (2011). Inferring cocaine flows across Europe: Evidence from price data. *Journal of Drug Policy Analysis, 4*(1), 1–18.
Desroches, F. J. (2007). Research on upper level drug trafficking: A review. *Journal of Drug Issues, 37*(4), 827–844.
Dietzler, J. (2013). On 'organized crime' in the illicit antiquities trade: Moving beyond the definitional debate. *Trends in Organized Crime, 16*(3), 329–342.
Ehleringer, J. R., Casale, J. F., Barnette, J. E., Xiaomei, X., Lott, M. J., & Hurley, J. (2012). 14C analyses quantify time lag between coca leaf harvest and street-level seizure of cocaine. *Forensic Science International, 214*(1–3), 7–12.
FATF/OECD. (2014). *Financial flows linked to the production and trafficking of afghan opiates*. Paris: Financial action task force/organisation for Economic Co-operation and Development.
Frontex. (2018). *Risk Analysis for 2018*. Warsaw: Frontex - European border and coast guard agency. https://frontex.europa.eu/assets/Publications/Risk_Analysis/Risk_Analysis/Risk_Analysis_for_2018.pdf.
Hickman, M., & Taylor, C. (2002). Estimating the prevalence of problematic drug use: A review of methods and their application. *Offprint from Bulletin on Narcotics* LIV (1 and 2).
Hughes, C. E., Chalmers, J., Bright, D. A., Matthew-Simmons, F., & Sindicich, N. (2012). Examining supply changes in Australia's cocaine market. *Drug and Alcohol Review, 31*(3), 263–272.
Johnson, T. P. (2014, 2014). Sources of error in substance use prevalence surveys. *International Scholarly Research Notices*, e923290.
Kilmer, B., & Hoorens, S. (2010). *Understanding Illicit Drug Markets, Supply-Reduction Efforts, and Drug-Related Crime in the European Union*. Product Page. 2010. http://www.rand.org/pubs/technical_reports/TR755.html.
Kilmer, B., & Pacula, R. L. (2009). *Estimating the size of the global drug market: A demand-side approach*. Product Page. http://www.rand.org/pubs/technical_reports/TR711.html.
Kilmer, B., Caulkins, J. P., Pacula, R. L., & Reuter, P. H. (2011). Bringing perspective to illicit markets: Estimating the size of the U.S. marijuana market. *Drug and Alcohol Dependence, 119*(1–2), 153–160.
Kilmer, B., Caulkins, J. P., Midgette, G., Dahlkemper, L., MacCoun, R. J., & Pacula, R. L. (2013a). *Before the grand opening: Measuring Washington State's marijuana market in the last year before legalized commercial sales*. Santa Monica, CA: RAND Corporation http://www.rand.org/pubs/research_reports/RR466.html
Kilmer, B., Taylor, J., Hunt, P., & McGee, P. (2013b). Sizing National Heroin Markets in the EU: Insights from self–reported expenditures in the Czech Republic and England. In F. Trautmann, B. Kilmer, & P. Turnbull (Eds.), *Further insights into aspects of the illicit EU drugs market*

(pp. 247–255). Luxembourg: Publications Office of the European Union http://ec.europa.eu/justice/anti-drugs/files/eu_market_full.pdf

Kilmer, B., Everingham, S. S., Caulkins, J. P., Midgette, G., Pacula, R. L., Reuter, P. H., … Lundberg, R. (2014). *What America's users spend on illegal drugs: 2000–2010*. Santa Monica, CA: RAND Corporation http://www.rand.org/pubs/research_reports/RR534.html

Kilmer, B., Reuter, P. H., & Giommoni, L. (2015). What can be learned from cross-national comparisons of data on illegal drugs? *Crime and Justice, 44*(1), 227–296.

Kleiman, M. A. R. (1992). *Against excess: Drug policy for results*. New York, NY: Basic Books.

Kleiman, M. A. R. (2004). *Illicit drugs and the terrorist threat: Causal links and implications for domestic drug control policy*, 24.

Kleiman, M. A. R. (2009). *When brute force fails: How to have less crime and less punishment*. Princeton, NJ; Woodstock: Princeton University Press.

Landesco, J. (1932). Crime and the failure of institutions in Chicago's immigrant areas. *Journal of the American Institute of Criminal Law and Criminology, 23*, 238.

Lippert, O., & Walker, M. (1997). *The underground economy*. Vancouver: The Fraser Institute. https://www.fraserinstitute.org/sites/default/files/UndergroundEconomy.pdf#page=33.

Louwage, F. E. (1951). Delinquency in Europe after World War II. *Journal of Criminal Law and Criminology, 42*(1), 53.

MacCoun, R., Kilmer, B., & Reuter, P. H. (2003). Research on drugs-crime linkages: The next generation. In *Drugs and crime: A research agenda for the 21st century*. Washington, DC: US Department of Justice https://www.ncjrs.gov/pdffiles1/nij/194616c.pdf

Madeira, L. F., Laurent, S., & Roque, S. (2011). *The international cocaine trade in Guinea-Bissau: Current trends and risks*. Noref working paper. Oslo: Norwegian peacebuilding Centre. http://noref.no/var/ezflow_site/storage/original/application/7563aa361160ef275ddd4f0812c6f41e.pdf.

Mazzitelli, A. L. (2011). The new transatlantic bonanza: Cocaine on highway 10. *Western Hemisphere Security Analysis Center*, March. http://digitalcommons.fiu.edu/whemsac/22.

Miron, J. A. (2001). *Violence, guns, and drugs: A cross-country analysis*. 2001. http://www.freerepublic.com/focus/news/713887/posts.

Moore, T. J., Caulkins, J. P., Ritter, A., Monagle, S., & Pruden, J. (2005). *Monograph No. 09: Heroin Markets in Australia: Current understandings and future possibilities*. DPMP Monograph Series. Fitzroy: Turning Point Alcohol and Drug Centre.

Ousey, G. C., & Lee, M. R. (2007). Homicide trends and illicit drug markets: Exploring differences across time. *Justice Quarterly, 24*(1), 48–79.

Paoli, L., Greenfield, V. A., & Reuter, P. H. (2009). *The world heroin market: Can supply be cut?* Oxford University Press.

Pedroni, P. L., & Verdugo, C. (2011). *The relationship between illicit coca production and formal economic activity in Peru*. IMF Working Paper 11/182. Washington, DC: International Monetary Fund. https://www.imf.org/external/pubs/ft/wp/2011/wp11182.pdf.

Pudney, S., Badillo, C., Bryan, M., Burton, J., Conti, G., & Iacovou, M. (2006). Estimating the size of the UK illicit drug market. In *Measuring different aspects of problem drug use: Methodological developments*. London: Home office.

Reuter, P. H. (2013). Are estimates of the volume of money laundering either feasible or useful? In B. Unger & D. van der Linde (Eds.), *Research handbook on money laundering* (pp. 224–232). Edward Elgar Pub.

Reuter, P. H. (2014). The mobility of drug trafficking. In LSE (Ed.), *Ending the drug wars. Report of the LSE expert group on the economics of drug policy*. London: The London School of Economics and Political Science.

Reuter, P. H. (2017). *Illicit financial flows and governance: The importance of disaggregation*. World Bank. http://pubdocs.worldbank.org/en/677011485539750208/WDR17-BP-Illicit-Financial-Flows.pdf.

Reuter, P. H., & Greenfield, V. A. (2001). Measuring global drug markets. How good are the numbers and why should we care about them? *World Economics, 2*(4), 159–173.

Reuter, P. H., & Kleiman, M. A. R. (1986). Risks and prices: An economic analysis of drug enforcement. *Crime and Justice, 7*, 289–340.

Reuter, P. H., & Majmundar, M. (2015). *Understanding the U.S. illicit tobacco market: Characteristics, policy context, and lessons from international experiences*. Washington: Committee on the Illicit Tobacco Market: Collection and Analysis of the International Experience; National Research Council. http://www.nap.edu/catalog/19016/understanding-the-us-illicit-tobacco-market-characteristics-policy-context-and.

Rhodes, W., & McDonald, D. (1991). *What America's users spend on illegal drugs*. Washington, DC: Executive Office of the President, Office of National Drug Control Policy.

Ryan, J., & Griffiths, P. (2013). *Profits dwarf drug responses*. 11–6. Anex Bulletin. Carlton: Anex. http://www.penington.org.au/wp-content/uploads/2016/09/Anex-Bulletin-Vol11-6.pdf.

Savona, E. U., & Mancuso, M. (2017). *Fighting illicit firearms trafficking routes and actors at European level. Final report of project FIRE*. Milano: Transcrime – Università Cattolica del Sacro Cuore. http://www.transcrime.it/pubblicazioni/fire-fighting-illicit-firearms-trafficking-routes-and-actors-at-european-level/.

Savona, E. U., & Riccardi, M. (2015). *From illegal markets to legitimate businesses: The portfolio of organised crime in Europe*. Trento: Transcrime – Università degli Studi di Trento. http://www.transcrime.it/pubblicazioni/the-portfolio-of-organised-crime-in-europe/.

Schelling, T. C. (1967). Economics and criminal enterprise. *The Public Interest*, (7), 61–78.

Suvantola, L., Favarin, S., Mehlbaum, S., Sahramäki, I., Savona, E. U., Spapens, T., & Kankaanranta, T. (2017). *Blocking the loopholes for illicit waste trafficking*. Tampere: Commission of the European Union - Police University College https://drive.google.com/file/d/1ItSzdolm0Gt4D7iw9XdlohxqvRa81h5I/view

Thoumi, F. E. (2002). Illegal drugs in Colombia: From illegal economic boom to social crisis. *Annals of the American Academy of Political and Social Science, 582*, 102–116.

Thoumi, F. E. (2005). The numbers game: Let's all guess the size of the illegal drug industry! *Journal of Drug Issues, 35*(1), 185–200.

Transcrime. (2015). *European outlook on the illicit trade in tobacco products*. Trento: Transcrime – Università degli Studi di Trento. http://www.transcrime.it/pubblicazioni/european-outlook-on-the-illicit-trade-in-tobacco-products/.

Tunnell, K. D. (1993). Inside the drug trade: Trafficking from the dealer's perspective. *Qualitative Sociology, 16*(4), 361–381.

UNODC. (2011). *Estimating illicit financial flows resulting from drug trafficking and other transnational organized crimes*. Research Report. Report. Vienna: United Nations Office on Drugs and Crime. http://www.drugsandalcohol.ie/16151/.

UNODC. (2015). *Drug money and opiate trafficking on the Balkan route*. Vienna: UNODC. http://www.unodc.org/unodc/en/frontpage/2015/November/drug-money-and-opiate-trafficking-on-the-balkan-route%2D%2Dfocus-of-new-unodc-report.html?ref=fs1.

Chapter 4
Data and Assumptions Behind the Application of the Flow-Network Approach to the Cocaine Trafficking

4.1 Introduction

The chapter describes the operational details of the methodology proposed to estimate the gross value added (GVA) and the illicit financial flows (IFFs) related to illicit physical transactions. The methodology combines insights from the good/monetary flow approach to the study of transnational trafficking (Paoli, Greenfield, & Reuter, 2009), along with data generation techniques developed in the field of criminal network analysis (Berlusconi, Aziani, & Giommoni, 2017; Boivin, 2013, 2014a; Chandra & Barkell, 2013; UNODC, 2015b) to provide a longitudinal and cross-sectional estimates.

The proposed methodology underpinning the estimate of gross value added has four steps. Each section of the chapter revolves around one step of the proposed methodology. The first step involves identifying the cocaine trafficking flows among countries by using information about seizures. The second step consists of sizing each national market. The third step deals with calculating the quantity of cocaine trafficked between any pair of countries by combining the estimates obtained by conducting the first two steps. The fourth section provides the final estimation of the economic value of drug trafficking in terms of GVA and IFFs related to physical illicit transactions.

The proposed methodology quantifies the GVA of cocaine markets by utilizing a method that aims to address, as far as possible, the numerous weaknesses in the available data and the fragility of certain assumptions. The resulting estimate is not without its limitations; nevertheless, it is a unique instrument with which to comprehend the distinctive characteristics of illicit markets. Furthermore, the cross-sectional and longitudinal nature of the estimates allows for their exploitation in panel data analyses aimed at evaluating crime reduction policies, which are absent in the extant literature. Moreover, it provides an important advancement in the production of any bottom-up estimate of IFFs. The exclusive focus on cocaine trafficking is functional to presenting in detail each of the multiple steps composing the methodology; on the

A. Aziani, *Illicit Financial Flows*, SpringerBriefs in Criminology,
https://doi.org/10.1007/978-3-030-01890-0_4

contrary, most methodologies in the literature lack the necessary level of detail, and thus provide less reliable estimates. Not all steps of the methodology can be adjusted to different transnational crimes or illicit markets by simply substituting data sources. Nonetheless, researchers applying the same estimation strategy in different contexts have to address the same challenges and formulate similar assumptions; and they should pay attention to the same shortcomings.

4.2 Constructing the Trafficking Network: Step 1

The global trafficking network, as per the methodology proposed by Boivin (2011), is built by using information from seizure cases. Original information on seizures can be retrieved from the IDS online databases of the UNODC (2014b, 2018), which cover the years since 1997, and from the IDS databases of the Drug Monitoring Platform (DMP), which is an online tool for collecting, monitoring, and sharing a wide range of drug-related data and which features an interactive online mapping resource. The availability of data on a specific drug trafficking route is adopted as the unique criterion for its inclusion in the network.

UNODC collects information on drug seizures (i.e., amphetamine-type stimulants (ATS), cannabis-type, cocaine-type, hallucinogens, opioids, sedatives, and tranquilizers) by inviting all United Nations member states to provide information on IDS through the Annual Report Questionnaire (ARQ) and the Drug Monitoring Platform (UNODC, 2016a). Member states are urged to transmit to the UNODC a variety of information on significant seizure cases, such as the date and the place of seizures, the type of drug, the seized quantity, the mode of transportation, and several other factors, including the origin, transit, and destination of the seized shipments, which are the most important for the construction of the trafficking network.

In general, the quantity of information provided on seizures of drug loads is more abundant than that provided on other aspects of drug trafficking and consumption. However, national institutions submit this information on a voluntary basis, and, as such, some countries may not report information. This may give rise to a lack of certain connections in the network, as well as potential bias in estimates (Boivin, 2011, 2013; UNODC, 2015b). To increase the completeness of the database, UNODC primarily complements seizure data made available to UNODC via the ARQ with data from other government sources, such as official national publications, as well as data provided by the Heads of National Law Enforcement Agencies (HONLEA). UNODC integrates its final databases also with data published by international and regional organizations, such as Interpol/ICPO, World Customs Organization (WCO), European Monitoring Centre for Drugs and Drug Addiction (EMCDDA), and the Inter-American Drug Abuse Control Commission (CICAD) (UNODC, 2016a).

There remain challenges when using information provided by the UNODC, because of gaps in the data and their varying quality, despite the fact that UNODC collects information from multiple sources. The irregularity and incompleteness in ARQ reporting by members may also result in the absence of seizure data for particular years. Further, submitted questionnaires are not always complete or comprehensive. Even if UNODC closely oversees data collection and performs several checks to improve data reliability, much of the data collected are subject to limitations and biases that UNODC are unable to fully solve. These issues undoubtedly affect the reliability, quality, and comparability of the available information.

Information on seizures allows for the identification of pairs of countries exporting and importing illicit goods with each other, as well as establishing the position of each country in the international trafficking network. At certain points, depending on the occurrence of the seizures, law enforcement agents are able to trace the movements of shipments between countries. For instance, the interception of a load bound for Canada on the border between Mexico and the United States suggests the existence of a path from Mexico to the United States and on to Canada (Boivin, 2013). In some cases, the dyad may be even more obvious; for example, if the seizure takes place on a commercial plane traveling direct from Argentina to Spain, then it would be reasonable to assume that cocaine routinely makes the same trip, especially if it is discovered on a passenger or in his/her luggage. In less simple cases, information on seizures can emerge later after more sophisticated investigations, or, alternatively, may remain unknown to law enforcement agencies (Boivin, 2011). The seizure case is worthless in terms of reconstructing the structure of the network, when information on the movements of drug loads is missing.

The transformation of available information into dyads is straightforward. It involves the origin, transit, and destination data being put into a relationship with the reporting countries, thus mapping the connection among those countries. By replicating the same procedure for all the countries, it is possible to map the entire network. As seen in the first example, a single seizure case can provide evidence of two dyads: Mexico-United States and United States-Canada. In the proposed methodology, the construction of the network adopts the perspective of importing countries. That is, information provided by exporting countries is used only to identify the connections of those countries that do not pass seizure information on to the UNODC (see Fig. 4.1). The preferential use of the information provided by importing countries allows for a reduction in the potential bias in estimates of the size of flows due to asymmetries in interception rates.

In total, with respect to cocaine trafficking in the years 1997–2014, UNODC's databases catalog 133,090 seizure cases. 35,102 of them provide useful information for identifying the international cocaine trafficking network. These seizure cases refer to 11,306 dyads. Interpolation leads to the estimate of the weight of 17,376 connections (1142 different ones) among 151 countries around the world, some spanning the entire period of 1997–2014, while others are identifiable for only 1 year (see Fig. 4.2). 39 of the 151 countries are located in Africa, 35 in the Americas, 34 in Asia, 40 in Europe, and 3 in Oceania. The structure of the network confirms the global dimension of the phenomenon, and thus justifies a global approach to studying it.

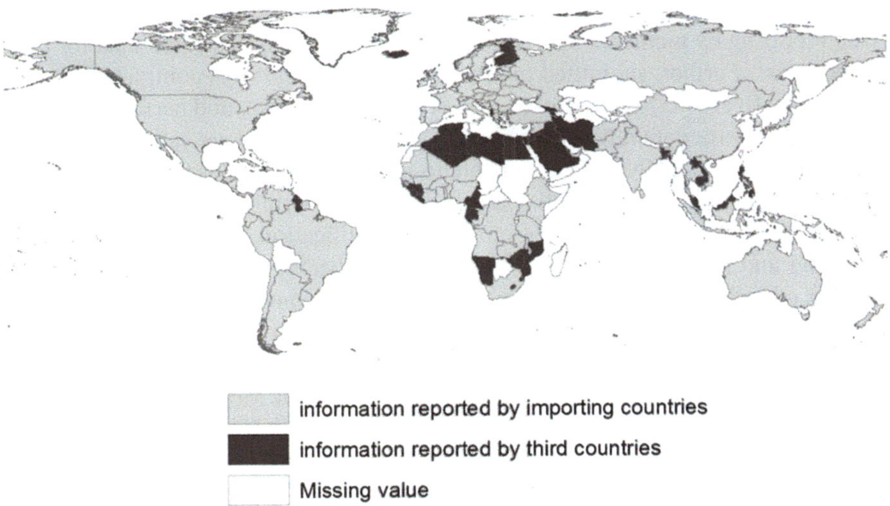

Fig. 4.1 Source of information on seizure cases.
Note: To mitigate the potential bias in estimates due to asymmetries in the effectiveness of interception efforts, the proposed methodology suggests relying primarily on information provided by the countries in which the drug load is entering. (Source: author's elaboration)

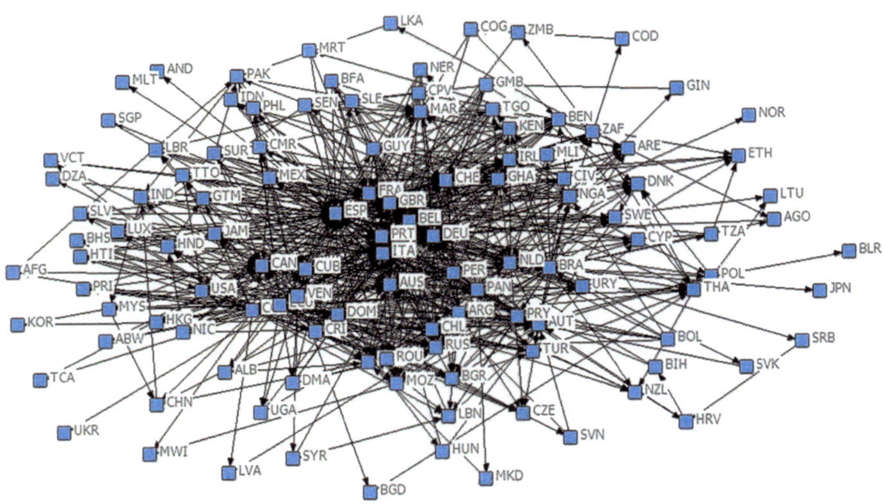

Fig. 4.2 Global cocaine trafficking network as emerging from the information on seizure cases.
Note: The network of 151 countries built on the basis of seizure cases (1997–2014) confirms the global dimension of cocaine trafficking and justifies a global approach to the estimate of related IFFs and GVA. (Source: author's elaboration)

4.2.1 Potential Sources of Bias

Law enforcement attention to trafficking issues varies among countries, as does the effectiveness of their actions. Economically developed countries tend to be more effective in intercepting illicit shipments than developing countries where there is widespread corruption. When it comes to weighting the dyads, disparities in the level of seizures are likely to inflate the relevance in transnational cocaine trafficking of those countries exporting cocaine to destinations that are characterized by effective border patrols. Conversely, the role of countries exporting to destinations where law enforcement is more relaxed would be unduly downsized. This bias is potentially severe when taking into consideration a global network in which interacting countries have extremely heterogeneous counter-drug policies, levels of corruption, and law enforcement agencies. The same reasoning applies to most transnational traffics as it is mainly due to interception and data-reporting capacities.

The preferential information provided by importing countries increases the robustness of the estimates of the weights of the shipments, albeit detrimentally affecting the number of observations and leading to the potential loss of specific connections. While for countries involved in large illicit flows, all major connections emerge when taking only their seizures into consideration, this might not be the case for more peripheral countries; given the lower number of seizures, the likelihood of missing some connections is far greater. Indeed, the reports from international organizations that are used to supplement actual data on seizures are often selective and tend to focus on the most used routes, thus overlooking minor connections. The centrality of the estimates of volumes for the entire analysis, allied with the minimum impact that the choices have on countries providing large amounts of information, gives credence to the adoption of this strategy.

Further potential biases may also stem from misunderstandings in the compilation of the IDS on the behalf of officials of the UN member states. With respect to the origin of drug shipments, UNODC's guidelines invite officers to indicate the "producing/manufacturing country" referring to "[...] countries where the drug crop was cultivated or the drug was manufactured" and the "country of departure" meaning the "[...] countries [...] that were the point of departure for drug traffickers, or unaccompanied shipments of drugs, reaching your country" (UNODC, 2015a, 10–11). The combination of this information should allow UNODC to provide a point of origin for drug shipments. Although on careful consideration, the two meanings are different, one can easily foresee occurrences when the terms are treated as synonymous with one another. The same form invites officers to provide information regarding transit and departure countries; the former means the last country through which the drug passed before entering into the country reporting the data, whereas the latter refers to the first country from which the drug shipments departed. Yet again, the two meanings are different, but just as before, the terms are often interpreted as synonyms.

Moreover, officers, on occasion, appear to simply report the last country to which they can track back the shipment, which, of course, can differ from the last country from which the cocaine actually flowed (Boivin, 2011). With respect to certain years and specific countries, data referring to origin and destination are clearly inverted; for example, there are cases of information provided by African countries which locate the origin as Europe and the destination as Colombia or Brazil. Methodically checking the information on each seizure case strengthens both the validity and richness of the analysis, but it cannot guarantee the complete reliability of the original information. Despite all its shortcomings, the UNODC database remains the best available option, because it provides conveniently accessed information unavailable anywhere else (Boivin, 2014b; Caulkins, 2007).

Finally, the economic feasibility of all the transactions identified is checked for trade prices adjusted for their purity level. The assumption is that both counterparts must gain from the trade (Caulkins & Bond, 2012; Reuter, 2014). Therefore, the structure of trade prices has to allow traffickers from the exporting country to sell the drug at a price higher than the price they paid for their loads. At the same time, traffickers who operate in the importing country have to pay a price that allows them to make a margin from selling the cocaine down the supply chain, or further within the international market. Whenever this criterion is not satisfied, the rationale is that the transaction will not occur; hence the final network does not include this specific dyad. Dyads conflicting with trade prices may emerge due to problems in the data (e.g., wrongly reported information on seizures, weak estimates of prices) and may represent minor flows which are not systemic but occasional. In both of these cases, it makes sense to exclude them from the network. The estimate of purity-adjusted trade prices is presented in the section describing the approach to the quantification of monetary values of cocaine trafficking.

4.3 Sizing the National Markets: Step 2

The second step in estimating the GVA generated by trafficking involves quantifying the amount of drug consumed and seized in the countries under analysis. Quantifying the consumption of cocaine is necessary to assess both the value of the market at retail level and the amounts of international shipments of cocaine. This methodology assumes that the quantity of cocaine entering a country in any given year corresponds to the sum of internal consumption, national seizures, and exports to third countries. The same approach can be applied to the estimate of amounts and values of shipments of other illicit goods.

The following subsections present the data and the methodology adopted to estimate the total consumption and the purity-adjusted seizures of the countries under analysis. The size of the exported loads depends on the structure of the trafficking network; therefore, its estimate is presented within the description of the method to size the flows in the next section.

4.3.1 *Calculating the Consumption*

In every country, the overall consumption of cocaine is obtained by combining the data on adjusted prevalence rates with the number of days that cocaine is typically consumed and the quantity of pure cocaine consumed per use-day by user type, as suggested by Kilmer and Pacula (2009), Frijns and van Laar (2013), and Kilmer et al. (2014). The adopted methodology makes it possible to obtain most-plausible consumption ranges rather than point estimates. These consumption estimates are produced using country-specific data for Australia, the United States, and several European countries, for which data are available. For all other countries, the estimate relies on country-specific prevalence and region-specific assumptions about days of consumption and quantities consumed. Several authors have utilized similar methods to produce estimates of national consumption of illicit substances, despite limitations pertaining to the uncertain reliability of part of the underlying data (Paoli, Greenfield, & Zoutendijk, 2013; Baldassarini & Sallusti, 2014; Giommoni, 2014; Kilmer et al., 2014).

4.3.1.1 Prevalence of Use and Number of Users

Producing estimates about the prevalence of use among the general population is thus the key opening task of most drug information systems. Various methods are available to collect information on prevalence rates; population surveys are the most common for the study of cocaine use and are available in a large number of countries. However, population surveys have well-known limitations with respect to validity and reliability and, in fact, tend to deflate the actual level of consumption (Johnson, 2014). An unwillingness to report, non-response by heavy users, and misreporting of frequency of use are the most common issues when dealing with expensive drugs such as cocaine (Kilmer, Reuter, & Giommoni, 2015).

A number of studies have asserted that respondents are unwilling to report their drug consumption because of the stigma associated with it (Richter & Johnson, 2001; Harrison, Martin, Enev, & Harrington, 2007). The scale of the underreporting is inversely related to the level of social condemnation and legal penalties associated with the specific psychoactive substance. Hence, tobacco smokers tend to be more honest than cocaine users, who, in turn, are more honest than heroin users. A veritable plethora of research has shown that even anonymous surveys on licit substances, such as alcohol and tobacco, tend to underestimate the actual consumption of these substances. Nonetheless, this is particularly true for more stigmatized substances. On the contrary, in environments where drug consumption may be perceived as admirable conduct, it has been found that respondents may exaggerate their substance use. For example, surveys of adolescents conducted in classroom settings, where peers may be aware of each other's answers, may lead to inflated results (Johnson, 2014). The propensity of people with low self-control to consume drugs and yet provide false information about their attitudes and behavior is another potential source of bias stemming from statistical estimates in survey-based research (Meldrum, Piquero, & Clark, 2013).

Secondly, surveys are conducted in a variety of different ways across different countries (e.g., self-administered paper-and-pencil or electronic questionnaires, telephone or face-to-face interviews). A number of studies have documented the dependence of survey findings on administration techniques. Survey modes that rely on respondent self-administration are found to obtain greater reports of drug use than those based on face-to-face interviews (Johnson, 2014; Turner et al., 2005). Discrepancies in the techniques of data collection across countries also impact negatively on cross-country analyses and estimates (Kilmer et al., 2015).

The third, and likely most severe, issue concerns non-response. High-using groups, in particular, have high non-response rates (Kilmer et al., 2015). This potential source of bias is due to the difficulties in reaching the relevant subpopulation of drug users in the original survey data, especially if the primary purpose of the survey is not directly related to the consumption of illicit substances, like most general censuses are. The number of intensive users is relatively small, thus requiring a large sample to intercept them. More problematically, surveys tend to overlook people who are in treatment or incarcerated, all of whom are expected to have higher prevalence rates (Hickman & Taylor, 2002; Parey & Rasul, 2015).

Indirect estimation methods (e.g., capture-recapture methods, multiplier methods, benchmark methods, event-based multipliers, truncated Poisson) are the other suite of techniques used to estimate the prevalence of cocaine use that scholars have developed to overcome the inherent issues with using surveys. Starting with a sample of drug users, the indirect methods identify the proportion of the targeted population with problematic use in the general population (Hickman & Taylor, 2002). These methods are rarely employed and do not allow the collection of information on the frequency of use.

UNODC and the EMCDDA are the primary providers of estimates on the prevalence of drug use among the general population. Prevalence data collected by both UNODC and the EMCDDA give priority to nationally representative households but come from a variety of sources and may be adjusted to account for age groups, geographical areas, youths or treatment surveys, and others to increase their comparability (UNODC, 2017; EMCDDA, 2015). Caulkins, Behrens, et al. (2004) provide further information, which affords the extension of the US time series.

Surveys are severely limited when it comes to estimating the prevalence of more marginalized forms of drug use, such as crack, which further complicates the production of reliable figures on the consumption of this substance (Fendrich & Xu, 1994; Lu, Taylor, & Riley, 2001). Problems in identifying key characteristics of the crack-using population also undermine other data gathering methods; for example, medical death certificates do not distinguish between powder cocaine and crack cocaine (Schifano & Corkery, 2008). Data on annual prevalence of cocaine use provided by UNODC includes and, in most of the cases, does not differentiate between different coca derivatives. Most other data on cocaine market are concerned specifically with cocaine salt. Since prices, purity levels, and patterns of consumption are different for powder cocaine and other coca derivatives, the use of generic prevalence rates thus raises a potential bias when other information specifically concerns cocaine salt; the higher the prevalence of cocaine in forms other than salt, the higher the bias.

The consumption of coca derivatives other than powder cocaine is not homogeneous across countries. The North American and European markets mainly concern cocaine powder. According to Fryer and his colleagues (2013), who constructed a "crack index" based on several proxies, in the United States crack consumption slowly declined after its peak at the end of the 1980s but still remained at 60–75% of its highest level in 2000. The prevalence of crack cocaine use in the United States has remained stable at around 0.6% of the population aged 12 and older through the 2000s, according to the adjusted results of a national survey (OAS, 2008). The consumption of crack cocaine is also present in most European markets, but it tends to be circumscribed to certain marginalized subpopulations in specific cities. Therefore, crack accounts for a small fraction of the overall market, with the United Kingdom and the Netherlands being notable exceptions (Pudney et al., 2006; Reid et al., 2012; Frijns & van Laar, 2013).

Crack cocaine ordinarily generates very little cross-border or long-distance trafficking, at least in Europe. This is due to the fact that crack tends to be manufactured from cocaine hydrochloride close to its retail and use locations (EMCDDA and Europol, 2010). Moreover, there are no substantial differences between the respective purity-adjusted prices of crack and cocaine salt (Caulkins, 1998; Kilmer et al., 2014). The similarity between the prices of these two substances reduces the distortions introduced by not considering all markets separately. With respect to these factors, most studies sizing cocaine markets jointly consider both salt and crack cocaine (e.g., Baldassarini & Sallusti, 2014; Kilmer et al., 2014; Giommoni, 2015).

In South America, people make use of other coca derivatives, such as *basuco* or *merla*. However, according to a survey based on 61,607 interviewees, which represented a total of 43 million people between the age of 15 and 64 from six South American countries, even in those countries where the consumption of these coca derivatives is more widespread, their market share remains marginal (UNODC, 2008).

Information on cocaine prevalence of use presents substantial uncertainty in every country in the world. Asian and African estimates, above all, remain tentative and have substantial levels of uncertainty. However, the two macro-areas are believed to account for a relatively small fraction of global cocaine consumption (UNODC, 2015c), with Africa accounting for around 5% and Asia around 3% (UNODC, 2011a). If this conventional wisdom is true, then errors in the sizing of African and Asian countries do not overly impact upon the calculation of the cocaine flows in relation to all other countries. Moreover, African markets tend to import cocaine directly from major South American players like Colombia and Brazil; accordingly, any bias in the estimate of the prevalence of African countries would be projected onto the masses imported by these countries without affecting estimates concerning other areas.

In some countries data on prevalence rates are produced annually, while in the majority of cases they are less frequent (e.g., roughly every 2–5 years) (Kilmer et al., 2015; UNODC, 2016b). Several developing countries, however, reported very few estimates during the surveyed period, while others failed to provide prevalence rates at all. In the absence of a precise function capable of describing the evolution of prevalence over time, missing data are estimated using a linear interpolation technique. The fact that, at a global level, the annual prevalence of cocaine use remained largely stable over the course of the period 1997–2014 legitimates the adoption of this strategy to deal with missing data (UNODC, 2016a). Average regional prevalence rates are used for the few countries not collecting any data required by UNODC as part of its attempt to estimate the global cocaine market.

An abundance of literature discusses the evolution of cocaine use initiation rates; contrary to the popular image of the entrepreneurial drug dealer who reels in new addicts through aggressive salesmanship, it is now clear that almost all first experiences are the result of being offered the drug by a friend or sibling (Caulkins, Behrens, Knoll, Tragler, & Zuba, 2004). The spread of drug use can be represented in terms of the diffusion of communicable diseases: that is, users are contagious, and people beside them may get infected (Paoli et al., 2009). However, there is little agreement about which factors impede initiation from spreading from friend to friend to the entire population.

Considering these dynamics, Caulkins, Behrens, et al. (2004) propound a model that enables the translation of historical initiation data into prevalence of heavy and light users, after having estimated a few parameters explaining the flow of consumers from low intensity of use to high intensity of use. Yet, when extending the production of estimates from the United States to countries with lower data availability, any straightforward replication of this type of model is unfeasible. The high interdependence of prevalence rates across years makes linear interpolation results a simple alternative to deal with gaps in the original data. Finally, multiplying the adjusted prevalence levels by the population aged between 15 and 64 generates the number of users per year for each country.

4.3.1.2 Dealing with Underreporting and Uncertainty in the Estimates

As already discussed, population surveys run into several difficulties: consumers may hide, may not be available for interview, and have reasons not to be honest when providing their answers. Furthermore, general surveys underrepresent heavy use consumers, who are more difficult to reach. Given that most of the countries included in this analysis were in a state of potential epidemic during the period considered, this source of bias is moderately attenuated (Kilmer & Pacula, 2009). It is different for countries such as the United States where the proportion of heavy users was probably large during the year covered by this review of available data. For these reasons, available data on prevalence rates should be viewed as conservative at best.

Firstly, in order to address the limitations of extant data on prevalence, the proposed methodology considers the lower and higher estimates available in the UNODC's databases along with the best estimate of the prevalence. The construction of a lower and upper estimate in each step of the methodology finally enables the generation of an upper and a lower estimate of the identifiable IFFs and of the GVA. The high uncertainty embodied in several data suggests considering the lower and upper estimates as indicators of the range within which the plausible value of profit is more likely to be, not its true possible extreme values nor a classic statistical confidence interval.

The proposed methodology corrects the number of users to account for underreporting as done in previous studies (Kilmer & Pacula, 2009). Even if researchers recognize underreporting as a major issue when estimating prevalence via population surveys, available data make it impossible to calculate a specific denial rate for each country. Consequently, a homogeneous correction parameter is applied to all countries. Following Kilmer and Pacula's (2009) approach, the best estimate of the number of users is multiplied by 1.5 so as to obtain an adjusted best estimate (see Fig. 4.3). This amounts to asserting that two thirds of cocaine consumers truly report their behavior, while a third of them disguise their consumption, which is similar to the findings of several of the aforementioned studies. These studies obtained an underreporting rate close to a third in different years, which suggests that the phenomenon may be relatively stable over time. However, it is important to note that

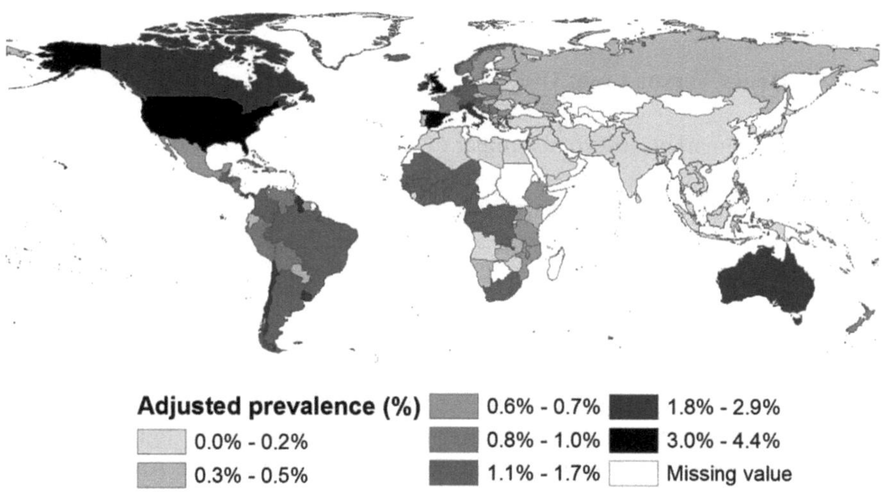

Fig. 4.3 Best estimate of the adjusted prevalence, 1997–2014 average.
Note: With different levels of reliability, it is possible to estimate the prevalence of cocaine consumption for a large part of countries of the world; countries completely lacking information on cocaine prevalence of use are likely to have small populations of consumers. European and North American markets, together with Australia, register the highest prevalence of cocaine use; the number of consumers is increasing in South American and Western African countries. (Source: author's elaboration on UNODC data)

the research for these studies was conducted in only two countries (i.e., the United States and United Kingdom), so that the underreporting rate may be significantly different in other contexts.

The proposed methodology takes the highest value between the double of the best estimate and the highest original estimate of the UNODC in order to determine the higher estimate of the adjusted prevalence rate. The lower estimate is equal to the lowest estimate of the UNODC when available and the original best estimate when it is not. Kilmer and Pacula (2009) and Kilmer et al. (2014) already proposed this construction of the lower (100% honest responses) and higher (50% of honest responses) bounds.

Despite UNODC's effort to homogenize the original estimates, national surveys are likely to be different in their effectiveness in depicting the true extent of cocaine consumption. This is because of the different methods on which they rely, the different levels of stigmatization, variations in rates of heavy and light users, and other reasons (de Leeuw, Hox, & Dillman, 2008). Consequently, the adjusted numbers of consumers are better than original estimates in describing the phenomenon at a national level, but do not increase the comparability of prevalence rates across countries. It should be said that these multipliers are tentative and not firm estimates and are likely to be improved upon when better information on underreporting of cocaine consumption is produced. Still, the introduction of these corrections permits the generation of estimates that are reasonably close to those already available in both peer-reviewed and grey literature.

4.3.1.3 Heavy Versus Light Users

In several drug markets, the total number of users is dominated by occasional users, while the relatively small share of heavy users accounts for the bulk of total consumption (Reuter, 1996; Kleiman, 2004). In their renowned study, Everingham and Rydell (1994) estimated that 22% of American cocaine users account for 70% of total consumption. According to a 2010 update, 18% of American cocaine users take cocaine more than once a week and account for two thirds of the total US consumption of cocaine (Kilmer et al., 2014). Other estimates, such as that by Anthony and Fries (2004), are available in the extant literature, and while figures vary from author to author, nobody questions the overall validity of Everingham and Rydell's (1994) observation. While studies concerning the distribution of light and heavy users in the consumer population have focused mainly on North America, more recently researchers have begun to conduct similar research in both several European countries (Frijns & van Laar, 2013; Škařupová, 2014) and Australia (AIHW, 2014), and they have obtained similar results.

Given the unequal consumption habits among different classes of consumers, a more accurate measurement of drug markets depends on the ability to estimate the size of these groups and to account in different ways for their specific behavior. Since estimates of the prevalence of use are based on general population surveys, data regarding frequency of use based on different targeted populations may inflate the overall estimates. In the proposed methodology, the estimate of the shares of light and heavy users relies on information from general population surveys, wherever reliable national estimates are available. In all of the countries that lack specific estimates, the distribution of heavy and light users is based upon information from third countries, which is in line with what Kilmer and Pacula (2009) and UNODC have done in several of their publications (see Fig. 4.4).

Due to the early and vast spread of cocaine consumption, the population of consumers in the United States is different from those in other countries; in fact, the United States is characterized by a larger share of experienced heavy users. Because of these specificities, a separation of North American estimates of consumption is recommended. At the same time, the contemporary importance of the topic, allied with a generalized sensibility toward data and statistics within North American culture, has culminated in an availability of data larger in the United States than in any other country. These data permit ad hoc estimates concerning the distribution of heavy and light users. Relying on the data and the model proposed by Everingham and Rydell (1994), Abt (2001), Caulkins, Behrens, et al. (2004), Kilmer and Pacula (2009), and Kilmer et al. (2014), it is possible to estimate the share of heavy and light users by year in the United States. The same estimate is then combined with the prevalence rates within Canada and Bermuda as well.

Data availability on European markets is not as rich as it is for the United States, although several general population surveys are available for a range of countries. In particular, in 2012, Trautmann, Kilmer, and Turnbull (2013) produced an online

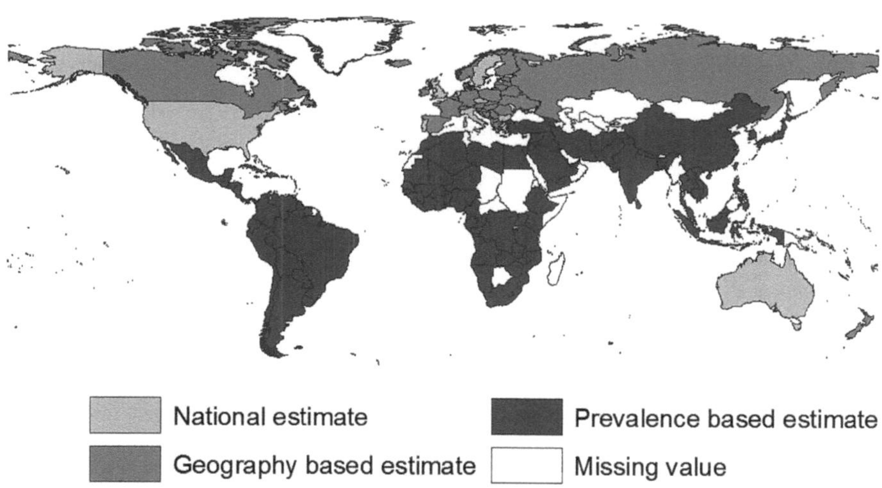

Fig. 4.4 Approach adopted to estimate the shares of heavy and light users.
Note: National estimates of the shares of heavy and light cocaine users are available for few countries in North America, Oceania, and in all European regions (i.e., Eastern Europe, Northern Europe, Southern Europe, Western Europe). It is possible to project these values to other countries belonging to the same macro region. Finally, by constructing strong assumptions on the basis of the epidemic cycle of drug consumption, estimation is made of the share of heavy and light users for many countries located in regions for which no data are available. (Source: author's elaboration)

Table 4.1 Proportions of cocaine users by user group and country in Trautmann et al. (2013) and as reaggregated according to Everingham and Rydell (1994)

		Infrequent	Occasional	Frequent
Bulgaria	Number	13	4	3
Trautmann et al.	%	65%	20%	15%
		Light		Heavy
Final estimate		79%		21%
Czech Republic	Number	54	8	5
Trautmann et al.	%	81%	12%	7%
		Light		Heavy
Final estimate		89%		11%
Italy	Number	69	20	9
Trautmann et al.	%	70%	20%	9%
		Light		Heavy
Final estimate		84%		16%
The Netherlands	Number	427	159	68
Trautmann et al.	%	65%	24%	10%
		Light		Heavy
Final estimate		83%		17%
Portugal	Number	17	6	5
Trautmann et al.	%	61%	21%	18%
		Light		Heavy
Final estimate		75%		25%
Sweden	Number	83	13	8
Trautmann, Kilmer, and Turnbull	%	80%	13%	8%
		Light		Heavy
Final estimate		88%		12%
England and Wales	Number	37	7	0
Trautmann et al.	%	84%	16%	0%
		Light		Heavy
Final estimate		95%		5%
All countries	Number	700	217	98
Trautmann et al.	%	69%	21%	10%
		Light		Heavy
Final estimate		83%		17%

Note: In Trautmann et al. (2013), infrequent users are those who use cocaine less than 11 days per year; occasional users are those who use cocaine between 11 and 50 times per year (at least once a month but less than once a week); frequent users are those who consume cocaine more than 50 days per year. To adapt these data to Everingham and Rydell's (1994) taxonomy, infrequent users and 61% of occasional users have been classified as light users; 39% of occasional users and frequent users have been classified as heavy users

survey targeting the general population and conducted face-to-face interviews with frequent (problem) users of cocaine. A sample of seven countries (see Table 4.1) was selected by the researchers. In light of this information, it is possible to subdivide the consumer population between heavy and light users in several countries and to obtain better data with which to infer the distribution within the entire area. To subdivide consumers according to the intensity of their consumption, my methodology adopts the modeling convention introduced by Everingham and Rydell (1994) and endorsed by many subsequent scholars. Those who use cocaine less than three times a month are defined as light users, while everyone else is considered a heavy user. Then, available information on frequency of use is adapted to estimate the weight of the two types of users in each country.

Trautmann et al.'s (2013) data gathering method has numerous limitations that the authors themselves discuss in their report, where they state that further research is needed to improve the data on the frequency of use of the less common drugs including cocaine. Accordingly, data on Italy are used to test estimates produced by Trautmann et al. (2013) because Italy is the only country included in the sample where national institutions have produced alternative estimates.

The 2003 Italian household survey reported that 78% of past year cocaine users had used cocaine once or less per month, 13% used cocaine between two and four times a month, 6% used cocaine between two and three times a week, and 4% used cocaine four or more times a week. Since frequency of drug use is likely to be higher among more marginalized groups, the results of these surveys underestimate the actual frequency of cocaine consumption. Nevertheless, the results of household surveys may be expedient when, as in the case of this methodology, data on prevalence are collected in the general population. That said, Italian observations do not exactly mirror the categories originally used by Everingham and Rydell (1994). Kilmer and Pacula (2009), who use these data in their study, propose two methods with which to translate these Italian data into Everingham and Rydell's scheme and then assume 17% to be the share of heavy drug users, while, given the dichotomy of the categories, light users correspond to 83% of the user population.

These estimates are consistent with those obtained using information provided by Trautmann et al. (2013) and, as such, corroborate the quality of the data despite the small numbers of interviewees. The results of this test also support the use of the punctual data provided by Trautmann et al. (2013) for the entire period under analysis. Indeed, even if the proportion of heavy and light consumers is known to change over time (Kraus et al., 2003; Caulkins, Pacula, et al., 2004), the limited available data concerning Italy do not show any significant evolution between 2003 and 2012.

In the past decade, the Australian Institute of Health and Welfare has produced a series of reports based on household surveys, which collect information from about 23,000/24,000 Australians about their tobacco, alcohol, and illicit drug use, attitudes, and opinions. As for other countries, it is then necessary to adapt information deriving from these general population surveys to the adopted categories of light and heavy users. People declaring that they consume cocaine either once or twice a year or every few months are cataloged as light users, while the share of people consuming cocaine at least once a month is, instead, divided between light and heavy users assuming a uniform distribution of frequency of use between 12 and 365. These calculations yield an estimated share of Australian light users of 88% in 2010 and 90% in 2013.

Approximating the distribution of light to heavy users of any country with the available information referring to countries in the same region, it is possible to estimate the distribution of heavy and light users for those countries where data are not yet available. It then becomes possible to use this fraction of past year users as parameters to determine the number of light and heavy users in each country using the country-specific annual prevalence rate for cocaine. In North America, all European regions, and Oceania, a minimum number of surveys have investigated the frequency of cocaine consumption within the general population. Data pertaining to the frequency of use are not available in Asia, Africa, or even Latin America, where a multitude of household surveys on drug consumption have been performed. The number of consumers living in these macro areas has monotonically increased during the past 20 years. The number and importance of the countries located in regions for which no specific surveys are currently available entails estimating a share of light and heavy users for these countries as well.

The present methodology takes into account the basic scheme of the epidemic cycle of drug consumption so as to identify a proxy for the distribution of the categories of consumers for Asian, Africa, Latina American, and Caribbean countries. Drug epidemic cycles are usually characterized by an initial phase in which, starting from a low level, drug initiation and use grow rapidly. Subsequently, initiation peaks, and shortly thereafter prevalence and the share of light users do the same (Winkler, Caulkins, Behrens, & Tragler, 2004). Thereafter, a portion of light users may escalate to heavy consumption, while total prevalence tends to decrease. The addiction problems stemming from the increasing share of heavy users then operate as a negative advertisement for the drug, which depresses initiation (Musto, 1973; Kleiman, 1992). At this point, the epidemic evolves into its endemic stage; the overall level of initiation and light drug use diminishes, and, consequently, heavy drug users increase their relative relevance (Hamid, 1992).

Taking this dynamic into consideration, the distribution of heavy and light users in the country with the most similar trend in the prevalence of use during the period under analysis is adopted as a proxy for countries in those regions where no surveys are available. This strategy relies firstly on the fact that scholars agree that infrequent users comprise the largest group in every market. Second, it is known that frequency of use, number of users, and the amount consumed per occasion of use are also related (Anthony & Fries, 2004). Nonetheless, assuming the same distribution of light and heavy users in countries with a similar trend in the prevalence of use remains a strong one. It will be possible to perform better estimates only when country-specific data on the frequency of cocaine use are available for a larger number of countries. Finally, by multiplying the shares of light and heavy consumers by country-specific annual adjusted prevalence rates for cocaine, it is possible to obtain the distribution of light to heavy users within the overall population of all of the respective countries.

4.3.1.4 Frequency of Use: Consumption Days for Heavy and Light Users

The frequency of drug use is the next element to be included in the estimate of the consumption of cocaine. But obtaining detailed information about the frequency of drug use in the past year or month is difficult. Misreporting the frequency of use is an additional problem associated with surveys: even though users admit their consumption, they often underreport their number of days of use in the past month or year (Kilmer et al., 2015). The extent of underreporting is, of course, almost completely unknown, which makes it difficult to correct the estimates for it (Kilmer et al., 2013). The proposed strategy is to readapt and merge estimates available in the literature into a single one to estimate the frequency of use of light and heavy users. In particular, the estimate produced by Kilmer and Pacula (2009) is combined with an original estimate based on the result of the survey developed by Trautmann et al. (2013). The resulting number of consumption days is then used to calculate the consumption of cocaine of all countries, excluding North America, where data on consumption per year of heavy and light users are directly available (Caulkins, Behrens, et al., 2004; Kilmer & Pacula, 2009; Kilmer et al., 2014).

The online survey by Trautmann et al. (2013) also investigates the typical number of consumption days of interviewed cocaine users (see Table 4.2). The authors proposed 12 different ranges of frequency of consumption and, for each category, indicated the number of responders who declared that particular frequency. People consuming cocaine between 1 and 20 times per year were labeled infrequent users; people declaring 21–50 consumption days were labeled as occasional users; finally, users using cocaine on more than 50 occasions in a year were considered to be frequent users. This methodology reclassifies infrequent users as light users and frequent users as heavy users; 69% of occasional users are then attributed to light users and the remaining 31% to heavy users (more than three times per month), as done for the estimate of the number of heavy and light users. Then, using the extremes of the ranges of the number of days for each group, we can construct a low and a high estimate of the number of use days for both light (4.8–10.3 days, midrange 7.6) and heavy users (93.0–122.8 days, midrange 107.9). The averages between these estimates and that produced by Kilmer and Pacula (2009) are then used to estimate the total consumption of cocaine in each country – excluding North America.

Not accounting for the plausible differences in the number of consumption days across countries inevitably introduces some biases into the final estimates, whose size and direction vary from market to market and are difficult to address. To mitigate this source of concern, as described in the next subsections, a regional correction factor is subsequently introduced to take into account the different amounts of cocaine consumed around the world, irrespective of the number of days in which it is used.

4.3.1.5 Consumption per Use Day by Light and Heavy Users

Grams consumed per use day, the third value necessary for performing consumption-based estimates, are also hard to determine. Almost all large surveys do not inquire about this aspect, while, simultaneously, most respondents are either ignorant about the exact weight of the cocaine they consume or are reticent about discussing it. Nonetheless, it is widely known that the amount of cocaine assumed per single occasion increases together with the frequency of use (Anthony & Fries, 2004;

Table 4.2 Estimate of the number of consumption days in the past 12 months

Trautmann, Kilmer, and Turnbull's categories	N. of use-days in the past 12 months, ranges	N. of respondents	Everingham and Rydell's categories	N. of use-days in the past 12 months, reaggregated ranges		Reaggregated N. of respondents	N. of use-days in the past 12 months, total by frequency (low)	N. of use-days in the past 12 months, total by frequency (high)	N. of use-days in the past 12 months, total by frequency (mid-range)
Infrequent	1–5	540	Light	1	5	540	540	2,700	1,620
	6–10	160		6	10	160	960	1,600	1,280
	11–20	115		11	20	115	1,265	2,300	1,783
				21	36	70	1,478	2,534	2,006
Occasional	21–50	102	*Sum, L.*			*885*	*4,243*	*9,134*	*6,688*
			Average, L.				*4.8*	*10.3*	*7.6*
			Kilmer and Pacula				*1.0*	*24.0*	*12.5*
			Adopted estimate L.				**3**	**17**	**10**
Frequent			Heavy	37	50	32	1,170	1,581	1,375
	51–80	42		51	80	42	2,142	3,360	2,751
	81–100	13		81	100	13	1,053	1,300	1,177
	101–150	19		101	150	19	1,919	2,850	2,385
	151–200	5		151	200	5	755	1,000	878
	201–250	7		201	250	7	1,407	1,750	1,579
	251–300	5		251	300	5	1,255	1,500	1,378
	301–350	2		301	350	2	602	700	651
	>350	5		350	375	5	1,750	1,875	1,813
			Sum, H.			*130*	*12,053*	*15,916*	*13,984*

	Average, H.				*93.0*	*122.8*	*107.9*
	Kilmer and Pacula				*85.0*	*169.0*	*125.0*
	Adopted estimate H.				**89**	**146**	**116**

Note: Author's elaboration on estimates by Trautmann et al. (2013), Everingham and Rydell (1994), and Kilmer and Pacula (2009). Data on infrequent, occasional, and frequent users are adapted to fit into Everingham and Rydell's taxonomy. After having estimated the number of consumption days using data from the online survey conducted by Trautmann et al. (2013), a final estimate is produced combining this estimate with that of Kilmer and Pacula (2009)

Frijns & van Laar, 2013). Authors have modeled these dynamics, but data capable of depicting the phenomenon are extremely rare. The literature also indicates that patterns of consumption of cocaine present important differences across the globe. In Africa, Asia, and Oceania the consumption of cocaine is generally on the increase, yet in these macro regions, consumers still tend to consume less cocaine than Europeans and Americans (UNODC, 2016a). To account for this aspect, it would thus be crucial to have reliable estimates.

Because of the dearth of data on the topic, available studies have mostly produced their estimates without considering national differences in the level of consumption per user (Kilmer & Pacula, 2009; UNODC, 2015b). The current methodology borrows from the extant literature the available estimates of the amount of cocaine consumed per use-day. The estimates are then exploited for the countries located in the different macro regions (i.e., North America, Europe, Oceania). In Asia, Africa, Caribbean, and Latin America, no national estimates of the consumption per occasion of use are available. To account for differences in the level of consumption in these regions, the methodology uses regional estimates of consumption per user. The described methodology affords a best estimate together with a lower and a higher estimate for the consumption of cocaine of heavy and light users.

Pudney et al. (2006) provide one of the few estimates of the average consumption per occasion of use per heavy and light consumers. In their study, the authors define as an intensive user someone who used cocaine in the previous week, while light users included everyone else. Their operational definition of heavy users does not exactly match up with Everingham and Rydell's (1994) definition that is adopted in this methodology – more than two occasions per month – but it is probably close enough to be adapted to it.

Pudney et al. (2006) and his colleagues proposed, in the context of the United Kingdom, an estimate of 0.80 raw grams per use-day for heavy users and 0.55 raw grams per use-day for light users. For both the categories, they posited a margin of uncertainty equal to 0.20 g upwards and downwards. Gossop and his colleagues (2006) conducted a survey among past-month cocaine users in both clinical and non-clinical settings in London, the results of which corroborated those of Pudney et al. (2006). Gossop's study showed that, among people who can be considered heavy users, the typical amount consumed is about 0.90 g per occasion; this finding corroborates the use of 0.80 ± 0.20 g as best estimate of the consumption of heavy users.

In their survey, Trautmann et al. (2013) investigate the grams of cocaine consumed on a typical consumption day in the aforementioned sample of seven European countries. Jointly considering all the seven countries, the authors proposed a mean estimate of 0.49 g of cocaine consumed on a typical consumption day for infrequent users (median 0.25 g), 0.82 g for occasional users (median 0.50), and 1.18 g for frequent users (median 1.00 g). Survey responses do not allow for country-specific estimates of the cocaine consumed on a typical consumption day per user group. However, the aggregated figures emerging from the survey confirm the validity of the estimate by Kilmer and Pacula (2009) regarding typical consumption amounts in European countries. The ranges 0.55 ± 0.20 and 0.80 ± 0.20 g may then be used to estimate the level of consumption in all European countries. The aforementioned Australian household survey provides the data for Oceania.

The UNODC (2010b) provided an estimate of the annual consumption per user, per year, per macro area during 2008. Because of this information, it is possible to calculate the relative differences in the consumption across areas and to use these differences to adjust the levels of consumption previously obtained for Africa, Asia, the Caribbean, and Latin America. Since the data of Pudney et al. (2006), Kilmer and Pacula (2009), and Trautmann et al. (2013) act as a proxy for European countries, the regional correction is the ratio between the consumption per user in Europe and the consumption per user of the region to which the specific country belongs. Given that UNODC presents annual consumption data as opposed to estimates of the volume of consumption per occasion of use, this correction also enables us to partially account for macro regional differences in the frequency of use (Fig. 4.5).

Like other information, data on quantity consumed per use-day are more abundant in the United States than any other country. Consequently, it is possible to produce an ad hoc estimate for the United States by exploiting the data and the model by Caulkins, Behrens, et al. (2004) and Kilmer et al. (2014). The emerging estimate based on US data is also adopted for Canada (see Fig. 4.6). Data are not equally rich in any other region.

Drug users cannot reliably report on the purity of the cocaine they consume; therefore, data on consumption per occasion of use refer to raw amounts of cocaine. Nonetheless, the *flow network* model requires adjusting raw masses for

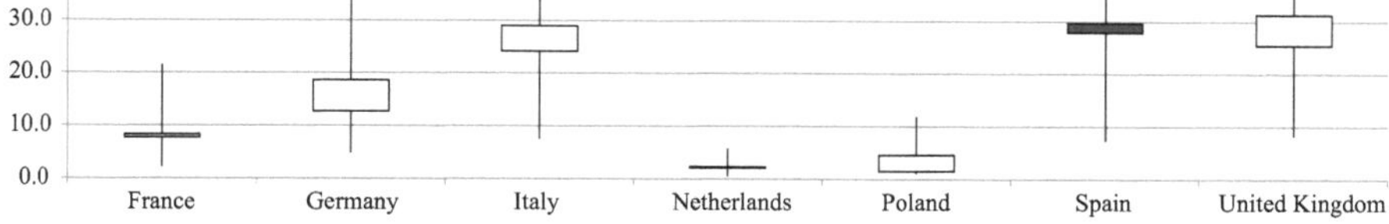

Fig. 4.5 Comparison with Kilmer and Pacula's (2009) estimate of adulterated cocaine consumption in 2005 (metric tons).
Note: The graph represents the best estimate of cocaine consumption in metric tons of adulterated cocaine produced by using the proposed methodology together with the best, low, and high estimates by Kilmer and Pacula (2009) for the seven European countries included within their study. The black lines indicate the range of the estimates by Kilmer and Pacula (2009). The boxes represent the discrepancies in the estimate between my best estimate and Kilmer and Pacula's (2009) best estimate. Kilmer and Pacula's (2009) estimate is higher for Germany, Italy, and the United Kingdom (light gray boxes) and lower for France, the Netherlands, and Spain (dark gray boxes). The estimates based on the proposed methodology fall within the boundaries of the highest and lowest estimate by Kilmer and Pacula for all the countries for which was possible to perform a comparison

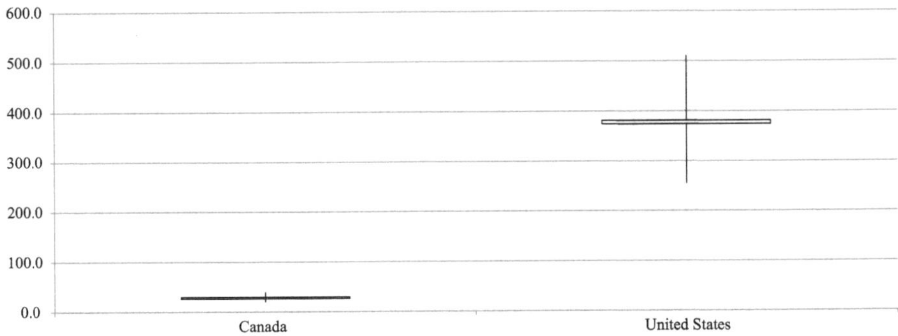

Fig. 4.6 Comparison between the estimates emerging from the proposed methodology and Kilmer and Pacula's (2009) estimate of cocaine consumption in 2005 in Canada and in the United States (metric tons).
Note: The graph represents the best estimate of cocaine consumption in metric tons of pure cocaine proposed by this methodology together with the best, low, and high estimates of Kilmer and Pacula (2009) for the United States and Canada. The black lines indicate the range of the estimates by Kilmer and Pacula (2009). The gray boxes represent the discrepancies in the estimate between this methodology's estimate and Kilmer and Pacula's (2009) estimate. Kilmer and Pacula's (2009) estimate is slightly higher for both the United States and Canada

purity levels. UNODC's *Delta ARQ* database provides national estimates of purity levels. Hence, by correcting for purity at retail level, the methodology allows for comparing masses across countries and along the supply chain while, simultaneously, introducing a country-specific correction.

4.3.1.6 Purity Adjustment of Consumption

Most drugs are not consumed in their pure form, and cocaine is no exception in this regard; it is usually mixed or cut with other substances before being used. Traffickers and dealers may mix additional substances with cocaine in order to inflate its volume and to complement or enhance the effects of the drug. Different substances are used, depending on the purpose of the cut. Consequently, most consumption estimates are also based on raw grams, as that is what consumers are able to report. Consumers are usually unaware of the purity of the substances they purchase and tend to base their judgment of quality on place of purchase, price per gram, and their administration modes (e.g., insufflation, inhalation), thus making surveys useless with respect to this issue (Paoli et al., 2009; Evrard, Legleye, & Cadet-Taïrou, 2010).

Since drug purity varies across countries, along the supply chain, as well as over time, it becomes necessary to adjust final estimates of total consumption for purity levels.[1] The correction for purity levels introduces national and temporal specificities into the estimates (i.e., the purity level itself) but, most importantly,

[1] North American markets constitute an exception; indeed, the methodology and the data underpinning this consumption estimate are different for this area, as they directly lead to purity-adjusted volumes which do not require further refinement.

allows for a comparison and a combination of masses and monetary values at different levels of the supply chain. Purity levels are fundamental for estimating the size of the drug markets and for understanding their functioning. Despite the centrality of this class of data for the comprehension of drug production and trafficking, complete purity series are not available in most countries.

Ideally, the Delta ARQ database of the UNODC (2014a) provides six estimates of the level of cocaine purity per country per year (i.e., minimum, typical, and maximum purity at street and at wholesale levels). It so happens that the UNODC releases the data without further testing its validity (Boivin, 2014b). Consequently, before using UNODC's data, it is necessary to check them for incongruities and errors in compiling. For the countries for which no data on purity of cocaine are available at retail level, purities may be imputed by using the average purity level of the region.

Original data come from national institutions, in particular, law enforcement agencies that estimate these figures using information from laboratories and cocaine shipment seizures in producer and transit countries, as well as information from the retail level through street seizures in consumer countries (UNODC, 2002; Mejía & Posada, 2008). The analysis of seizures occurring at retail level introduces a high level of variability even when comparing only a specific year, a specific place, or a specific transaction size (Caulkins, 1995). Moreover, as shown by several researchers, there is importance within-country variation with respect to purity. Using average measures fails to take accurate account of these differences. Nonetheless, it is common practice to use estimates of the overall level of drug purity in a market when it comes to estimating its size or value (Giommoni, 2014; Kilmer & Pacula, 2009; Reuter & Greenfield, 2001).

The transformation of the raw quantities into pure quantities poses additional problems. Indeed, the purity of cocaine consumed may present some differences between light and heavy users. This is due to the fact that heavy users tend to purchase product of a higher quality, due to the fact that they rely on selected sellers, or because they are more discerning consumers and can thus inspect the product (Kilmer et al., 2014; Anthony & Fries, 2004). Despite this reasoning and anecdotal evidence about potential differences in the level of purity for the two categories of consumers, by all accounts, information about the levels of purity of cocaine consumed by light and heavy users does not exist, which means that this aspect cannot be included within the final estimates. However, using the lower and higher levels of purity of cocaine at retail level makes it possible to integrate this consideration into the analysis.

4.3.2 Calculating Purity-Adjusted Seizures

The adoption of the demand-side estimate approach requires summing national seizures to the estimate of cocaine consumption to finally size national markets. Overall, data on total seizures of cocaine for a given country in a given year are more robust than most other data pertaining to drug markets. UN member states

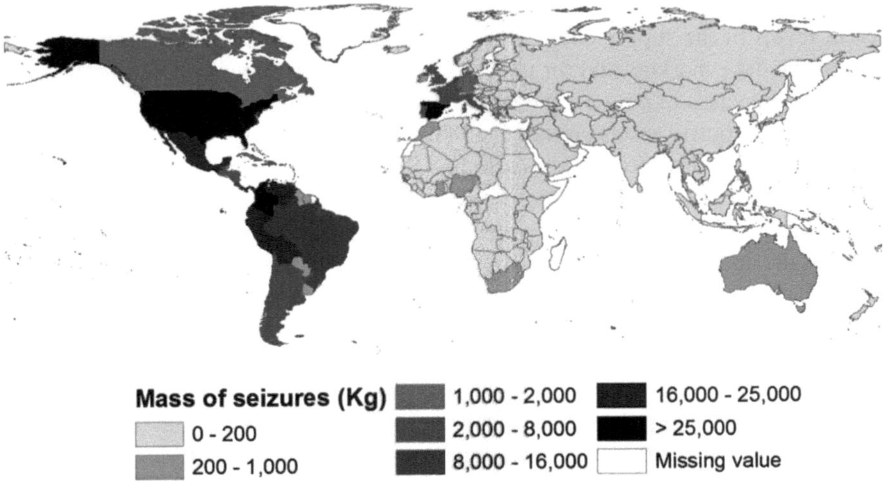

Fig. 4.7 Mass of seizures, average 1997–2014.
Note: Not surprisingly, cocaine interceptions are particularly important in the production countries. Out of Andean area, Venezuela, Mexico, the United States, Spain, and Panama stand out for the size of their cocaine seizures, which suggests their centrality for the trafficking of cocaine and/or as large destination markets. Despite the increased importance of the Western African trafficking route, the vast majority of African countries declare very low interceptions of coca derivatives. (Source: author's elaboration on UNODC data)

should report amounts of seized drugs on a yearly basis. Since not all countries report their seizures, the UN supplements their databases with information provided by a number of other institutions. The combination of national data and information from these key international law enforcement agencies makes the UNODC database the most complete for dealing with global seizures (see Fig. 4.7). Nonetheless, reported seizures may not be fully representative of the actual amount of drug intercepted in a country. First, seizures may not be fully announced, or complete information may not be carefully recorded or transmitted to international institutions. Second, anecdotal evidence indicates that total figures may be inflated by double counting of interceptions by different national law enforcement agencies, as well as by different countries (UNODC, 2010a).

4.3.2.1 Purity Adjustment of Cocaine Seizures

Reported seizures are for impure cocaine, and the amount of pure cocaine seized is determined by taking into account the purity of seizures, which varies considerably within/across countries and according to the level of the supply chain. Overall, national seizures are divided into three hypothetical levels of the supply chain (i.e., international trade, intermediate distribution, and retail level) in order to take account of different purity levels along the supply chain. The relative importance of the seizures occurring at the different levels of the supply chain is determined by observing the distribution of the seizures as reported by the law enforcement agencies to the UNODC. If the seizure has a mass smaller than 1.0 kg, then it is assumed to concern low-level retail trafficking; if the seizure has a mass between 1.0 and 10 kg, then it is considered to concern intermediate distribution; finally, if the seizure load is more than 10 kg, then it is assumed to concern high-level trafficking. UNODC (2015b) developed these weight ranges by adjusting and combining information provided by Rossi and Ricci (2009) and the EMCDDA (2011), exploiting them to adjust the purity of seizure cases of heroin. These ranges are intended to accommodate the characteristics of different national drug markets. In reality, the drug traded at different stages of the supply chain is likely to differ from country to country according to the total mass of coca derivatives circulating in the country. However, precise information on the size of transactions is hard to collect (UNODC, 2015b).

Over the last few years, the average size of seizures of cocaine has been about 5.0 kg. This value is the highest of all drugs, but it also represents a decline since the past decade from 6.2 to 4.6 kg (UNODC, 2015c). These differences may stem from variations in trafficking *modus operandi* across time and with respect to different drugs, as well as developments in law enforcement strategies and priorities, but they also may be a consequence of improved reporting of small seizure cases in certain regions. Today, the available information does not allow for the disentangling of the relevance of these explanations. Both an underreporting of smaller seizure cases and an increase in the precision of reporting minor seizures would compromise the reliability of the estimate. In any case, small seizures are contemporaneously more likely to be left out of reports and less influential for the calculus of the three categories, thus prospecting a certain efficacy of the methodology despite the possible omissions.

After attributing seizure cases to one of the three levels of the national supply, the relative weight of the three groups is then calculated for each county. For example, the share of seizures occurring at retail level is equal to the ratio between the sum of seizure cases whose mass is smaller than 1 kg and the total of seizure cases. After estimating the volume of seizures occurring at each step of the supply chain, it is possible to adjust each of them for the corresponding estimated purity level and to sum them again to obtain the total of purity-adjusted seizures. The two-step procedure of (1) calculating the relevance of the categories using seizure cases (IDS) and then (2) projecting them on the total of seizures (ADS) is necessary because national institutions do not report all seizure cases to the UNODC. Therefore, the sum of seizure cases (IDS) does not correspond to the total amount of seizures in a country (ADS).

4.4 Sizing the Drug Flows: Step 3

It is then necessary to weigh the quantity of drug flowing through each connection. This requires (1) estimating the relative weight of each link with respect to the other links connecting the same importing country and (2) transforming into masses the relative weight of each connection. To estimate the parameter representing the relative weight of the dyad between the two countries, the volume of the seizures from one country to another is divided by the total volume of seizures concerning the importer. To accomplish the second step, the size of flows is calculated, starting from the estimated size of the importing market. The model assumes that every country imports a mass of cocaine equal to the sum of consumed cocaine, national seizures, and exports. In turn, the volume of exports by country depends on the imports of all other countries in the network. Therefore, it is possible to calculate backwards the volumes trafficked between each pair of countries, once the relative importance of each connection and the mass of the imports of the final destination markets are known.

4.4.1 Weighting the Dyads

Information on seizure cases provided by the UNODC always includes the mass of the seizures. These data permit estimation of the amount of trafficking between two countries with respect to others. The basic rationale is that the relative masses of seizures may be indicators of the relative masses of drug flows (Berlusconi et al., 2017; UNODC, 2015b). In its simplest form, the idea is that, considering any importing country (e.g., Morocco), if seizures of drugs flowing from a specific country (e.g., Algeria) are more abundant than seizures along another connection (e.g., drug flowing from Mauritania), then drug trafficking along the first connection (e.g., Algeria-Morocco) is likely to be more copious than along the second one (e.g., Mauritania-Morocco). In reality, factors other than the actual amount of the flow influence this relationship; one route may be more successfully targeted by law enforcement, or it may be that the data reporting systems of countries along the first route are more efficient than the data reporting systems of countries along the second route (UNODC, 2015b).

It follows that it is preferable to estimate the relative weight of drug flows on a country-by-county basis. This methodology divides the amount of seizures intercepted while flowing between two countries by the total seizures referring only to the importing country, thus obtaining an estimate of the relative relevance of that connection for that specific importing country. In the vast majority of cases (86% considering the years 1997–2014), only information provided by the importing country enter into the calculation of the weight of the links, in turn reducing the biases of different law enforcement and reporting systems. Even within a single country, however, law enforcement agencies may be more concerned about certain specific routes or means of transport, thus inflating the perceived importance of these connections. This kind of situation, however, is unlikely to last over time in the absence of structured corruption schemes, because the imbalance among the law enforcement actions would induce traffickers to move their shipments to less controlled paths.

Law enforcement agencies mainly intercept cocaine hydrochloride, but they also seize coca leaves, coca paste, cocaine base, and crack cocaine. Volumes of different coca derivatives are converted into cocaine hydrochloride volume equivalents according to conversion rates, as proposed by the UNODC (2010a, 2011b), in order to make them comparable in terms of psychoactive substance masses. Seizures are not purity-adjusted when used to construct the network. Different drug flows originating from different countries are unlikely to have exactly the same level of purity; not accounting for purity levels may inflate the relevance of flows occurring between downstream countries, where cocaine is likely to be cut more. However, since information on seizures refers to coca derivatives entering the same country during the same year, it is reasonable to expect these differences not to be dramatic. The methodology does not consider seizures that may reenter the global market because of misconduct in public office. UNODC (2015b) makes the same assumptions when estimating the mass of opiates moving along the Balkan route.

One shortcoming of this approach is that the interception of particularly large loads may distort the estimates if they are far from being proportional to actual drug flows. While for land and air routes, this is rarely the case because volumes are smaller, it may happen with interceptions on sea routes, whose shipments are usually larger. To fully disentangle the extent to which larger seizures depict larger shipments or luckier operations is not possible; therefore, the use of moving averages helps in reducing the risk of distortion produced by particularly massive seizure cases in a specific year. For every year, the final estimate of the relative relevance of the specific connection is provided by the ratio between the 3-year moving average of the mass of seizures between a specific dyad and the moving average of total seizures relative to the importing country. Seizure volume enters into the calculus of the moving average with a weight that halves the values referring to the previous and next year with respect to the one of the estimate.

4.4.2 Combining Information on National Markets with Network Structure

By combining the network of trafficking with the size of the cocaine market in each country, it is possible to estimate the quantity trafficked through each link. The model assumes that every country imports a mass of cocaine equal to the sum of consumed cocaine, national seizures, and exports. In turn, the volume of exports by a country depends on the imports of all other countries in the network. It is therefore possible to calculate backwards the volumes trafficked between each pair of countries, once the relative importance of each connection and the volume of the imports of the final destination markets are known.

Part of the cocaine consumed in a given year is likely to have entered its final market the previous year. However, all available data, with the exception of seizure cases, are annual, which makes it extremely challenging to estimate the share of cocaine consumed in a given year which has been imported prior to that year. The use of moving averages partially relaxes the rigidity of the annual boundaries; further studies should develop methods to address this issue in a more sophisticated manner.

4.5 Estimating the Economic Value of Drug Trafficking and the Related IFFs: Step 4

By exploiting the information and the estimates on consumption, seizures, and structure of the network with a supply chain model and prices, it is now possible to obtain the estimate of the GVA produced in each country. The next subsection presents available estimates on prices, recalls the modeling of the drug trafficking supply chain, and describes adopted methodology to combine and use them. The following four subsections delineate how it is possible to estimate the GVA at each step of the supply chain and, finally, the IFFs related to the transnational trafficking (i.e., import and export) of cocaine.

4.5.1 Supply Chain and Prices

This operative methodology divides the cocaine supply chain into three main blocks or components: high/international level, intermediate/distribution level, and retail level. Illicit prices at each stage of the supply chain are valuable data for scholars attempting to analyze drug markets (Costa Storti & De Grauwe, 2009). However, the correct use of data on drug prices requires a comprehension of the contextual issues in which the same data have been generated, whether that be the gathering method or the problematic behind it (Caulkins, 1994, 2007). Drug markets, indeed, have peculiarities that make them different from any other market, such as the high variability of product quality, or the strong spatial variations of prices (Kleiman, 1992).

With respect to prices in final markets, the principal difficulty is that it is not possible to rely on information collected from buyers. Consumers cannot report a reliable price on a standardized unit; rather, they only know how much they spend on some quantity of drug, the actual potency of which is ordinarily unknown. This fact introduces a major obstacle because the range of pure gram prices at a retail level is huge. Prices vary enormously both between and within nations, as well as across time (Reuter, 2009). With these obstacles in mind, it is worth mentioning the three data sources of price data, as indicated by Caulkins (2007). The first one is synthesis reports by government agencies; the second is self-report by users; the third, and most widely used by scholars, is transaction-level data. Law enforcement agencies carefully record data on transactions while conducting their operations within illicit drug markets. These records may contain purity levels, prices, and quantity, which can be used for research purposes.

UNODC's online databases provide six levels of prices per country (i.e., minimum, typical, and maximum price at both street and wholesale levels) for most of the countries in the world. In addition, farm-gate prices are available for main producing countries (UNODC, 2016b). UNODC collects its price data from the *ARQ* and supplements these data with other sources such as DAINAP, EMCDDA, and government reports. Hence, by checking all the publications of the *World*

Drug Report, it is possible to increase the availability of data for some countries, and, in turn, have a more complete time series (see Fig. 4.8).

Data reported by the UNODC, much like data on drug prices in general, have neither the accuracy nor the depth of data on legal commodities. The UNODC is also not capable of fully assessing how data were collected and how reliable they were. Although improvements have been made over the years, a number of law enforcement bodies have not yet established a regular system for collecting price data (UNODC, 2016b). Despite these problems, authors have observed that UNODC's data on prices display broad phenomena and trends that match well with what one would expect both over time and across countries.

The current methodological approach checks the meaningfulness of available prices by comparing street level and wholesale prices, and it estimates missing data on prices by applying basic interpolation techniques as was done for missing data on purities. In order to make the quantities comparable, all the prices are purity-adjusted. By combining the estimates of the prices of cocaine with the corresponding estimates of purity, the proposed approach produces six estimates of purity-adjusted prices per country per year, one for each estimate of prices provided by the UNODC.

Finally, six original estimates of purity-adjusted prices for each country, one for every transaction included in the schematization of the cocaine supply chain, are produced by combining the different purity-adjusted prices. These purity-adjusted prices are named "international price," "average importing price," "average exporting price," "wholesale price," "distribution price," and "retail price." "Average

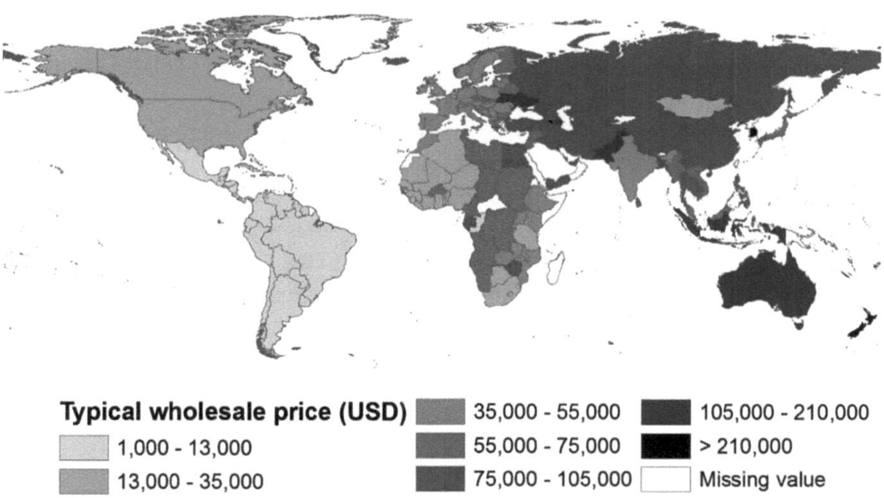

Fig. 4.8 Typical "wholesale price" as reported by the UNODC, average 1997–2014.
Note: As expected, wholesale prices of cocaine increase the further we go from the production countries; prices in several Western African countries contribute to confirming the importance of this corridor to reach Western and Central European markets. On the contrary, longer journeys and higher related risks cause wholesale prices to be high in most Asian and Oceanian countries. (Source: author's elaboration on UNODC data)

importing price" refers to the average price per kilogram of cocaine loads entering a country. Conversely, "average exporting price" indicates the average price that international traffickers operating in a given country are able to collect when they ship cocaine to the next country of the trafficking network. "International price" is the price at which an international transaction takes place between two specific countries. Therefore, the estimate of both "average importing price" and the "average exporting price" depends on "international price." "Wholesale price" is the typical price at the point of transaction between high-level international traffickers and intermediate distributors, who operate at the national level. "Distribution price" indicates the purity-adjusted price at which national distributors sell a kilogram of cocaine to local retailers. "Retail price" is simply the typical price at which final consumers purchase cocaine from their dealers.

The first three prices (i.e., "international price," "average importing price," and "average exporting price") are relational, that is, their value depends on the combination of estimates of prices in more than one country and on the specific connections of the trafficking network. The other three prices instead concern relationships between actors active within the same country (see Box 4.1). The main idea behind the estimate of these purity-adjusted prices is to interrelate all available price estimates, both in the international trafficking network and along the national supply chains. Regardless of the actual volumes at which these transactions typically occur, the estimate of profit relies on purity-adjusted prices for a kilogram of cocaine.

Box 4.1: Trading Price Estimates

This box describes the calculi behind the estimates of the prices proposed by this methodology in order to estimate cocaine trafficking related GVA and the IFF compensating the transnational shipments of cocaine.

"International price" (IP_{ijt}) (i.e., the typical price per kilogram of cocaine flowing into country i from country j in year t) is the minimum purity-adjusted wholesale price of the importing country i ($padjPR\_m\_ws_{it}$), if the minimum purity-adjusted wholesale price of the importing country i is higher than the minimum purity-adjusted wholesale price of the exporting country j ($padjPR\_m\_ws_{jt}$). If instead, the minimum purity-adjusted wholesale price of the importing country i ($padjPR\_m\_ws_{it}$) is not higher than the minimum purity-adjusted wholesale price of the importing country j, then the "importing price" (IP_{ijt}) is the average of the typical purity-adjusted wholesale price of the importing country i ($padjPR\_t\_ws_{it}$) and the minimum purity-adjusted wholesale price of the exporting country j ($padjPR\_m\_ws_{jt}$):

$$\left[IP_{it} = \left[padjPR\_m\_wh_{it} \geq padjPR\_m\_wh_{jt}\right] \Rightarrow padjPR\_m\_wh_{it};\ \left(\overline{padjPR\_t\_wh_{it}; padjPR\_m\_wh_{jt}}\right)\right].$$

"Average importing price" (AIP_{it}) (i.e., the average price per kilogram of cocaine entering into country i in year t) is the weighted average of the prices at import of countries i (IP_{ijt}), which imports cocaine from J countries. Specific importing prices (IP_{ijt}), referring to the transactions with country j, are weighted according to the size of loads flowing from that specific country (j) (I_{jit}):

$$\left[AIP_{it} = \sum_{j=1}^{J} IP_{ijt} \cdot I_{jit} / \sum_{j=1}^{J} I_{jit} \right].$$

"Average exporting price" (AXP_{it}) (i.e., the average price per kilogram of cocaine leaving country i in year t) is the weighted average of importing prices (IP_{kt}) registered by the K countries importing cocaine from country i. Specific importing prices (IP_{kit}), referring to the transactions with country k, are weighted according to the size of loads flowing into that specific country (k) (I_{kit}):

$$\left[AXP_{it} = \sum_{k=1}^{K} IP_{it} \cdot I_{kit} / \sum_{k=1}^{K} I_{kit} \right].$$

"Wholesale price" (WP_{it}) (i.e., the average price per kilogram of cocaine purchased by national-intermediate distributors in year t) is the average of minimum ($padjPR\_m\_wh_{it}$) and typical ($padjPR\_t\_wh_{it}$) purity-adjusted prices at wholesale level:

$$\left[WP_{it} = \overline{\left(padjPR\_m\_wh_{it}; padjPR\_t\_wh_{it} \right)} \right].$$

"Distribution price" (DP_{it}) (i.e., the typical price per kilogram of cocaine purchased by local retailers in year t) is the average of maximum purity-adjusted prices at wholesale level ($padjPR\_m\_wh_{it}$) and highest price between minimum purity-adjusted prices at street level ($padjPR\_m\_st_{it}$) and typical purity-adjusted price at wholesale level ($padjPR\_t\_wh_{it}$):

$$\left[DP_{it} = \overline{\left(padjPR\_M\_wh_{it}; \left[padjPR\_m\_st_{it} \geq padjPR\_t\_wh_{it} \right] \Rightarrow padjPR\_m\_st_{it}; padjPR\_t\_wh_{it} \right)} \right].$$

"Retail price" (RP_{it}) (i.e., the typical price per kilogram of cocaine purchased by final consumers) is the average of typical ($padjPR\_t\_st_{it}$) and maximum ($padjPR\_M\_st_{it}$) purity-adjusted prices at street level:

$$\left[RP_{it} = \overline{\left(padjPR\_t\_st_{it}; padjPR\_M\_st_{it} \right)} \right].$$

In the three main producing countries, project specialists of the *Sistema Nacional de Monitoreo*, supported by UNODC, collect monthly data on prices of sun-dried coca leaf, coca base, and cocaine. The UNODC publishes these prices together with other data obtained from the field in the volumes of the *Crop Monitoring Reports*. This list of publications supplements data in the *Delta ARQ* database with additional information on prices. In particular, farm-gate prices of cocaine and, alternatively, minimum registered prices of cocaine are used as costs to calculate profits of international traffickers of cocaine in Bolivia, Colombia, and Peru.

Data available in the UNODC's databases may present some differences with respect to the data originally reported by national law enforcement officers; these discrepancies are mainly due to currency conversions made by UNODC. Indeed, UNODC directly presents the data in USD equivalents, in order to facilitate their use and comparability. At the same time, comparisons of prices from different years need to be made with caution, since part of the variations may be due to changes in the exchange rates as opposed to prices actually observed in the market. The final estimate of the GVA and its main component are adjusted by the *Price level ratio of PPP conversion factor (GDP) to market exchange rate* developed by the World Bank, which increases the comparability of data across countries and longitudinally. The use of this specific adjustment factor allows for simultaneous account to be taken of the differences in the evolutions of the currency exchange rate across countries and the actual value of money in the particular country.

The combination of the original estimates of prices and volumes obtained by the estimate of the size of national markets, as well as information emerging from the *flow network* model, makes it possible to calculate the gross value added generated by cocaine trafficking for each country. Cocaine trafficking total GVA is the sum of the profit emerging from high international trafficking, from drug distribution at the national level, and from cocaine retailing. IFFs related to transnational cocaine trafficking correspond, instead, to the value of the masses of cocaine entering and leaving any given country.

4.5.2 GVA at Retail Level

GVA at retail level refers to the GVA generated by selling cocaine to consumers, which is estimated by calculating the difference between revenues at retail and costs incurred by dealers purchasing cocaine from national distributors. Consumers pay the dealer the cocaine "retail price," while dealers purchase cocaine from intermediate distributors at the "distribution price." The calculation of revenues at retail level is the most classic one: cocaine consumption is multiplied by purity-adjusted prices at retail level. The model assumes that law enforcement actions are able to intercept part of the cocaine circulating at retail level, as discussed in a variety of literature (e.g., Reuter & Kleiman, 1986; Everingham & Rydell, 1994). Retail dealers have to buy an amount larger than the one they sell to consumers; hence, they purchase from intermediate distributors a volume equal to consumption plus seizures at retail. The amount of seizures occurring at retail level is calculated by combining information on the size of seizures and the total level of seizures registered in the country.

Several simplifications with respect to reality characterize the estimate of GVA at retail level. It is common practice among cocaine retailers to offer quantity discounts to habitual clients (Caulkins & Padman, 1993). Therefore, the relevant price for the calculation of revenues at retail should not simply be the most widespread price of the typical unit of purchase but, rather, should account for quantity discounts. Available data does not permit us to understand the extent to which published retail prices reflect these dynamics, thus not allowing for introducing these refinements into the estimates.

Especially in consumer countries, price is not strongly related with purity when controlling for transaction size (Reuter & Greenfield, 2001). Authors explain this by stressing that illicit drugs are experience goods (Caulkins, 2007). That is to say, buyers pay a price according to their expectation of the quality of the substance they are buying, which is based upon observable information like the size of the purchase, location, and other factors. However, especially during the first transaction, sellers can deceive consumers about the quality of the product (Caulkins & Reuter, 1998; Mejía & Posada, 2008). Often, wholesale transactions also take place without any assessment of the purity being performed (Reuter & Caulkins, 2004). A weak correlation between prices and purity levels might suggest a low level of standardization in transaction at retail level and a resultant inability of typical/average data accurately to reflect the phenomenon. Moreover, it is not possible to state the direction of the eventual bias due to the quality of these data. Despite these limitations, authors adopting a global perspective for the study of drug trafficking have little choice but to work with the data available to them at that particular time.

Thirdly, people who are primarily involved in drug dealing in order to finance their own habit may provide their labor in exchange for the drugs they consume, or they may consume a portion of the drug that they purchase from intermediate distributors (Johnson, 2003). In both these cases, the final price that they pay for cocaine is below the typical purchase price paid by other consumers.

The final issue concerns cocaine received by consumers, either as a gift from friends or in exchange for services (Taylor & Potter, 2013). However, the practice is more common for less expensive drugs, such as methamphetamines and marijuana than it is for cocaine. Moreover, people sharing cocaine have purchased it. Because of this, the inclusion of these revenues in the final estimate is coherent with the assumptions of the model. All together, these considerations suggest that the overall estimate of GVA at retail level may underestimate the actual values.

4.5.3 GVA at National Distribution Level

At an intermediate-distribution level, drug traffickers manage large quantities of drugs domestically, connecting international traffickers to local retailers (Pearsons & Hobbs, 2001). While the presence of actors occupying intermediate positions in the supply chain is evident within even relatively small countries (Caulkins et al., 2016), it would be possible to redistribute to the higher and lower levels of the supply chain costs and revenues referring to the intermediate level of distribution. Despite this, inclusion in the model of an intermediate level between large-scale cocaine trafficking and retail level has been made in order to increase the model's coherence with the available literature and provides more elements for further analysis of the economic dimension of cocaine trafficking.

The difference between the value of the sale to retailers active in the country and the cost of purchasing products from high-level international traffickers ultimately determines the GVA at the intermediate-distribution level. The mass of cocaine that intermediate actors sell to local retailers is equivalent to the mass consumed plus seizures taking place at a retail level. Revenues at this level are equal to the sum of these masses times the "distribution price" that retailers pay to procure the cocaine from distributors. The costs for distributors are equal to the mass of cocaine that they purchase from high-level traffickers multiplied by the "wholesale price." In turn, the proposed approach is to assume that the cocaine purchased by distributors is equal to the sum of internal consumption, seizures at the retail level, and half of seizures at distribution level. The proposed approach includes only half of the costs of the mass intercepted at the intermediate level in its estimate of the costs for distributors, in order to account for the fact that the highest risks for traffickers come from transactions. If seizures are more likely to occur during transactions, in the absence of further information, it is prudent to attribute half of the burden of the lost goods to sellers and the other half to buyers.

4.5.4 GVA at Transnational Trafficking Level

High-level international trafficking refers to the traffic of large loads across national boundaries, and their distribution to intermediate distributors in destination markets, according to the conceptualization provided by FATF/OECD (2014) and UNODC (2015b). Revenues for high-level traffickers arise from both the trade of cocaine with other countries connected in the trafficking network and from the sale of cocaine to national distributors. Value of imports is obtained by multiplying imported volumes with the average of the "importing price"; in the same way, the value of the exports is a product of exported volumes and the average "exporting price." The proposed approach estimates both imported and exported masses in relation to the model presented in the Sect. 4.4.

For any given country, revenues from international trafficking are assumed to make up two thirds of the value of exports of cocaine and one third of the value of imports. The necessity to subdivide revenues related to international trafficking among importers and exporters in such a rough manner is a consequence of the substantial lack of information on the nationality of actors taking part in cocaine trafficking in each country. Even if scholars have closely documented the prominent role of some groups, such as Colombians, Italians, Mexicans, Cubans, Nigerians,

Turks, etc., in specific countries, it is not possible to develop meaningful estimates for all the countries of the network due to the available empirical data.

Revenues from drug sales to intermediate distributors are gained by multiplying "wholesale price" and sale mass, which, in turn, is equal to the sum of national consumption, seizures at retail level, and half of the seizures at an intermediate level. Both high-level traffickers and national distributors manage volumes of drugs compatible with intermediate level of trafficking, because they trade in cocaine in these masses among each other. Since available information does not allow for a more comprehensive understanding of which of the two categories suffers the costs of the seizures, the methodology splits the burden equally between both groups.

The estimate of the GVA does not assess costs such as those for transportation, guard services, and bribes. The methodology assumes that the margins of traffickers include the monetary value of these ancillary services. In any case, the literature indicates that these costs are relatively low in comparison to other dimensions of the business. Small groups can easily move large quantities of drugs and earn millions of dollars in rewards. Revenues within high-level trafficking are the difference between the two forms of revenues and these aforesaid costs.

4.5.5 GVA as Baseline to Estimate IFFs Related to ML of Cocaine Trafficking Proceeds

The sum of GVA at retail, distribution, and transnational trafficking level constitutes a potential base from which to estimate the IFFs related to the ML of illicit proceeds. The total sum of GVAs is an improvement with respect to the estimates of illicit proceeds exploited in the past to estimate transnational ML and IFFs through the use of the *Walker Gravity Model*. Yet greater detail and robustness in estimation of the monetary size of the cocaine industry does not seem to be enough to produce reliable estimates of IFFs related to the ML of these criminal proceeds. As outlined in the second chapter of this book, many further questions have to be answered before understanding how much money is transferred abroad because of ML purposes. In particular, it would be crucial to understand how many actors are active in the trafficking industry, what is their propensity to save, invest, and consume, and to what extent their laundering behavior exploits international threats and vulnerabilities.

In the absence of research and information on these topics, assumptions could be formulated to produce some estimates. It might be reasonable to assume that large-scale operators are able to generate higher profits and that consequently GVA at international level is going to be laundered abroad to a larger extent than GVA at distribution level which, in turn, would be transferred abroad to a larger extent than GVA at retail level. While retail accounts for the majority of overall profits made in the drug industry, at least in consumer markets, retail markets are characterized by a multiplicity of small actors who generate small profits and consequently small IFFs. To understand the direction of the IFFs, it could be possible to assume that ML behaviors mimic the practices of legal actors or that suspicious transactions are indeed good proxies for undetected IFFs.

Clearly, more research would be needed on the supply side of drugs, specifically on how large- and small-scale operations handle their finances. The reality is that nowadays the things that we do not know are much more than the things that we can credibly model. The extent to which researchers can rely on assumptions like the one mentioned in the previous paragraph depends on the geographic and temporal scopes of their research and estimates and, most importantly, of their final aim. At the moment, it is implausible to produce sound, comprehensive, and precise estimates of the IFFs related to the ML of illicit proceeds generated by traffickers. However, if the purpose of the exercise is to gain an idea of the overall order of magnitude of such IFFs, to compare IFFs estimated in the same manner for different illicit activities, or to investigate the relationship of these IFFs with certain specific factors as for example the transparency of the financial system of a country, the proposed approach based on the calculi of the GVA may prove beneficial as starting point.

4.5.6 IFFs Related to the Transnational Import and Export of Cocaine

The IFFs that this methodology aims directly to estimate are those related to the physical importing and exporting of drugs in a country; once the GVA at trafficking level has been estimated, the estimate of the IFFs directly related to cocaine trafficking is straightforward. Each international purchase of cocaine generates an outward IFF corresponding to the mass of cocaine coming from that specific country as determined by the *flow network* model multiplied by the "international price," which is the typical purity-adjusted price per kilogram of cocaine flowing between the two countries in a specific year. Conversely, every international sale of drug loads generates an inward IFF. The estimate of the inward IFF related to the sale of cocaine at the international level is given by the mass of cocaine flowing from one country to another multiplied again for the specific "international price" characterizing the relationship between these two countries.

Given the FNA, each inward IFF for a country corresponds to an identical outward IFF for the country from which the cocaine originates. Differently from the estimate of the GAV at transnational level, here there are no assumptions to be made about the distribution of the revenues among criminals coming from one country, the other, or a third one. The modeling of the transnational trafficking network allows for estimation of the IFFs related to drug shipments for each country providing an indication of the origin or destination of the drug load. Once again, however, it should be borne in mind that the real economy and financial relationships operate on different levels. A drug load moving from Venezuela to the Netherlands might suggest a financial transaction going in the exact opposite direction; that payment is the compensation for the drug shipment. Nonetheless, Dutch traffickers may move money not from the Netherlands but from a third country where they have a bank account. In the same manner, Venezuelan criminals may prefer to receive their payment in a different country offering them more security or the opportunity to hide their illicit activities better.

4.6 Conclusion

Today, the traditional categorization of nations as producer, consumer, and transit countries is no longer in vogue (Gratius & Palacios, 2012). Latin America, the Caribbean, Europe, not to mention Western Africa, and Central Asia are all regions where it is known that illicit drugs are consumed, produced, and transited (UNODC, 2017). Yet, as expected, the estimate indicates that GVA at retail level is higher in countries with both a largely installed base of consumers and relatively high retail prices, such as the United States or the United Kingdom. By comparison, in countries at the beginning of the trafficking routes, such as Colombia or Venezuela, the GVA at the trafficking level accounts for the largest share of the total GVA, especially if they have numerous naval connections with lucrative final markets. In the same vein, outward IFFs related to drug shipments are larger for countries at the beginning of the transnational supply chain of cocaine – the ones which export larger amounts of drug – and for well-known trafficking countries along the Caribbean coast and for European point of entry; these countries tend to combine large shipments with higher prices than Andean countries. Conversely, applying the proposed methodology, the main consumer countries in North America and Western Europe register most significant outward IFFs.

That said, it is important to stress that the proposed estimates of both the GVA and the IFF related to the transnational shipments of drug have specific limitations which must be taken into account when interpreting the results. First, even if one accepts the assumptions required to reconstruct the cocaine trafficking network and the size of national cocaine markets, the mobilized data have important limitations with respect to both their numerosity and their quality. The illegality of the cocaine market itself makes it extremely difficult to collect reliable information on a variety of crucial features, such as the number of users or prices. Data collection and validation issues are amplified when extended to cross-country analyses. Hence, although estimates may truly reflect differences in cocaine markets between countries, this may also be a consequence of countries' idiosyncratic data collection methods.

It is therefore evident that estimating the size of illicit drug markets is a challenging task. Moreover, moving away from an approach based on the number of users, expenditure, quantity consumed, seizures, or areas under cultivation to other approaches does not resolve all of the potential problems, because all of the methods described have their respective limitations and uncertainties. The impossibility of solving all of these issues results from the fact that the principal difficulties are not conceptual in nature. Uncertainty tends not to emerge from sampling variability, and therefore cannot be managed through statistical methods; rather, the problem is mainly with the available raw data. Unreliable answers to questionnaires and lack of information about the sophistication or otherwise of clandestine labs are just two of the possible shortcomings of attempts to study hidden markets and illicit behaviors. Consequently, the best strategy with which to estimate the size of any illicit market depends on the availability of data, on the specific dimension of the market under analysis, and on the final purpose of the estimate.

In this regard, it is important to stress that all of the results emerging from the proposed methodology should be considered as tentative rather than conclusive. Stronger data on seizures, per user consumption, stockpiles, etc., would allow a more rigorous refinement of the figures generated by the proposed methodology. At the same time, there is sufficient room to improve the management of missing data and tighten the rationale underlying certain steps of the network/flow model, such as the lack of relationship between seizures and consumption, the distribution of profit among traffickers from different countries, and the cost incurred by traffickers.

Still, the proposed methodology has the necessary level of detail to be ameliorated when better data will become available or when we achieve better understanding of the functioning and structure of the cocaine industry. The methodology has already the potential to provide useful information on IFFs related to the real-economy side of transnational drug trafficking. Even without reconciling these estimates with ML practices, the figures emerging from the proposed approach may prove useful in the design and evaluation of policies targeting the predicate offenses behind IFFs. Finally, with all the necessary calibrations, the details of the methodology described in this chapter can be readjusted to produce estimates of the IFFs related to other transnational crimes, from the trafficking of cigarettes to that of firearms.

References

Abt. (2001). *What America's users spend on illegal drugs*. Cambridge, MA: Abt Associates Inc.

AIHW. (2014). *National drug strategy household survey detailed report 2013*. Canberra, ACT: Australian Institute of Health and Welfare http://www.aihw.gov.au/alcohol-and-other-drugs/ndshs-2013/

Anthony, R., & Fries, A. (2004). Empirical modelling of narcotics trafficking from farm gate to street. In *Bulletin on narcotics* (Vol. LVI). Vienna, UNODC https://www.unodc.org/pdf/bulletin/bulletin_2004_01_01_1_Art1.pdf

Baldassarini, A., & Sallusti, F. (2014). *Estimating illegal drug flows in Italy: A statistical approach*. Presented at the 8th ISSDP conference, Rome.

Berlusconi, G., Aziani, A., & Giommoni, L. (2017). The determinants of heroin flows in Europe: A latent space approach. *Social Networks, Crime and Networks, 51*, 104–117.

Boivin, R. (2011). *Le monde à l'envers: analyse de la structure du trafic transnational de drogues illicites*. Montréal: Université de Montréal https://papyrus.bib.umontreal.ca/xmlui/handle/1866/6068

Boivin, R. (2013). Drug trafficking networks in the world-economy. In *Crime and networks*. London/New York, NY: Routledge http://erdr.org/textes/boivin.pdf

Boivin, R. (2014a). Macrosocial network analysis: The case of transnational drug trafficking. In A. J. Masys (Ed.), *Networks and network analysis for defence and security, Lecture Notes in Social Networks* (pp. 49–61). Springer International Publishing, New York.
Boivin, R. (2014b). Risks, prices, and positions: A social network analysis of illegal drug trafficking in the world-economy. *The International Journal on Drug Policy, 25*(2), 235–243.
Caulkins, J. P. (1994). *Developing price series for cocaine*. Santa Monica, CA: Rand Corp http://www.rand.org/content/dam/rand/pubs/monograph_reports/2007/MR317.pdf
Caulkins, J. P. (1995). *Estimating elasticities of demand for cocaine and heroin with DUF data*. Pittsburgh, PA: Carnegie Mellon University.
Caulkins, J. P. (1998). *Is crack cheaper than (powder) cocaine?* Santa Monica, CA: RAND Corporation http://www.rand.org/pubs/reprints/RP671.html
Caulkins, J. P. (2007). Price and purity analysis for illicit drug: Data and conceptual issues. *Drug and Alcohol Dependence, Behavioral and Economic Perspectives in Drug Abuse Research, 90*(Supplement 1), S61–S68.
Caulkins, J. P., Behrens, D. A., Knoll, C., Tragler, G., & Zuba, D. (2004). Markov chain modeling of initiation and demand: The case of the US cocaine epidemic. *Health Care Management Science, 7*(4), 319–329.
Caulkins, J. P., & Bond, B. M. (2012). Marijuana price gradients implications for exports and export-generated tax revenue for California after legalization. *Journal of Drug Issues, 42*(1), 28–45.
Caulkins, J. P., Disley, E., Tzvetkova, M., Pardal, M., Shah, H., & Zhang, X. (2016). Modeling the structure and operation of drug supply chains: The case of cocaine and heroin in Italy and Slovenia. *The International Journal on Drug Policy, 31*, 64–73.
Caulkins, J. P., Pacula, R. L., Arkes, J., Reuter, P. H., Paddock, S., Iguchi, M., & Riley, J. (2004). *The price and purity of illicit drugs: 1981 through the second quarter of 2003*. Washington, DC: RAND Corporation http://www.whitehousedrugpolicy.gov/
Caulkins, J. P., & Padman, R. (1993). Quantity discounts and quality premia for illicit drugs. *Journal of the American Statistical Association, 88*(423), 748–757.
Caulkins, J. P., & Reuter, P. H. (1998). What price data tell us about drug markets. *Journal of Drug Issues, 28*(3), 593–612.
Chandra, S., & Barkell, M. (2013). What the price data tell us about heroin flows across Europe. *International Journal of Comparative and Applied Criminal Justice, 37*(1), 1–13.
Costa Storti, C., & De Grauwe, P. (2009). Globalization and the price decline of illicit drugs. *International Journal of Drug Policy, 20*(1), 48–61.
de Leeuw, E. D., Hox, J. J., & Dillman, D. (Eds.). (2008). *International handbook of survey methodology* (1st ed.). New York, NY/London: Routledge.
EMCDDA. (2011). *Pilot study on wholesale drug prices in Europe*. Lisbon: European Monitoring Centre for Drugs and Drug Addiction.
EMCDDA. (2015). *European drug report 2015. Trends and development*. Lisbon: European Monitoring Centre for Drugs and Drug Addiction http://www.emcdda.europa.eu/publications/edr/trends-developments/2015
EMCDDA and Europol. (2010). *Cocaine: A European Union perspective in the global context, EMCDDA–Europol Joint Publications, 2*. Luxembourg: European Monitoring Centre for Drugs and Drug Addiction, Europol http://www.emcdda.europa.eu/publications/joint-publications/cocaine_en.
Everingham, S. S., & Rydell, C. P. (1994). *Modeling the demand for cocaine*. Santa Monica, CA: RAND Corporation http://www.rand.org/pubs/monograph_reports/MR332.html
Evrard, I., Legleye, S., & Cadet-Taïrou, A. (2010). Composition, purity and perceived quality of street cocaine in France. *International Journal of Drug Policy, 21*(5), 399–406.
FATF/OECD. (2014). *Financial flows linked to the production and trafficking of afghan opiates*. Paris: Financial Action Task Force/Organisation for Economic Co-operation and Development.
Fendrich, M., & Xu, Y. (1994). The validity of drug use reports from juvenile arrestees. *International Journal of the Addictions, 29*(8), 971–985.

Frijns, T., & van Laar, M. (2013). Amphetamine, ecstasy and cocaine: Typology of users, availability and consumption estimates. In F. Trautmann, B. Kilmer, & P. Turnbull (Eds.), *Further insights into aspects of the illicit EU drugs market* (pp. 183–242). Luxembourg: Publications Office of the European Union http://ec.europa.eu/justice/anti-drugs/files/eu_market_full.pdf

Fryer, R., Heaton, P., Levitt, S., & Murphy, K. (2013). Measuring crack cocaine and its impact. *Economic Inquiry, 51*(3), 1651–1681.

Giommoni, L. (2014). The retail value of the illicit drug market in Italy: A consumption-based approach. *Global Crime, 15*(1–2), 27–50.

Giommoni, L. (2015). Illicit drugs market. In E. U. Savona & M. Riccardi (Eds.), *From illegal markets to legitimate businesses* (pp. 43–56). Trento: Transcrime – Università degli Studi di Trento http://www.transcrime.it/pubblicazioni/the-portfolio-of-organised-crime-in-europe/

Gossop, M., Manning, V., & Ridge, G. (2006). Concurrent use of alcohol and cocaine: Differences in patterns of use and problems among users of crack cocaine and cocaine powder. *Alcohol and Alcoholism, 41*(2), 121–125.

Gratius, S., & Palacios, D. (2012). *Europe and Latin America: Combating drugs and drug trafficking*. Brussels: European Parliament – Directorate-General for External Policies http://www.europarl.europa.eu/RegData/etudes/etudes/join/2012/457107/EXPO-AFET_ET(2012)457107_EN.pdf

Hamid, A. (1992). The developmental cycle of a drug epidemic: The cocaine smoking epidemic of 1981–1991. *Journal of Psychoactive Drugs, 24*(4), 337–348.

Harrison, L. H., Martin, S. S., Enev, T., & Harrington, D. (2007). *Comparing drug testing and self-report of drug use among youths and young adults in the general population*. Rockville, MD: Substance Abuse and Mental Health Services Administration, Office of Applied Studies.

Hickman, M., & Taylor, C. (2002). Estimating the prevalence of problematic drug use: A review of methods and their application. *Offprint from Bulletin on Narcotics, LIV*(1 and 2), 15–32.

Johnson, B. D. (2003). Patterns of drug distribution: Implications and issues. *Substance Use & Misuse, 38*(11–13), 1789–1806.

Johnson, T. P. (2014). Sources of error in substance use prevalence surveys. *International Scholarly Research Notices, 2014*, e923290.

Kilmer, B., & Pacula, R. L. (2009). *Estimating the size of the global drug market: A demand-side approach*. Product Page. http://www.rand.org/pubs/technical_reports/TR711.html.

Kilmer, B., Caulkins, J. P., Midgette, G., Dahlkemper, L., MacCoun, R. J., & Pacula, R. L. (2013). *Before the grand opening: Measuring Washington State's marijuana market in the last year before legalized commercial sales*. Santa Monica, CA: RAND Corporation http://www.rand.org/pubs/research_reports/RR466.html

Kilmer, B., Everingham, S. S., Caulkins, J. P., Midgette, G., Pacula, R. L., Reuter, P. H., … Lundberg, R. (2014). *What America's users spend on illegal drugs: 2000–2010*. Santa Monica, CA: RAND Corporation http://www.rand.org/pubs/research_reports/RR534.html

Kilmer, B., Reuter, P. H., & Giommoni, L. (2015). What can be learned from cross-national comparisons of data on illegal drugs? *Crime and Justice, 44*(1), 227–296.

Kleiman, M. A. R. (2004). *Illicit drugs and the terrorist threat: Causal links and implications for domestic drug control policy*. CRS Report for Congress, p. 24.

Kleiman, M. A. R. (1992). *Against excess: Drug policy for results*. New York, NY: Basic Books.

Kraus, L., Augustin, R., Frischer, M., Kümmler, P., Uhl, A., & Wiessing, L. (2003). Estimating prevalence of problem drug use at national level in countries of the European Union and Norway. *Addiction (Abingdon, England), 98*(4), 471–485.

Lu, N. T., Taylor, B. G., & Riley, K. J. (2001). The validity of adult arrestee self-reports of crack cocaine use*. *The American Journal of Drug and Alcohol Abuse, 27*(3), 399–419.

Mejía, D., & Posada, C. E. (2008). Cocaine production and trafficking: What do we know? *Borradores de Economia* 444. Banco de la Republica de Colombia. http://ideas.repec.org/p/bdr/borrec/444.html.

Meldrum, R. C., Piquero, A. R., & Clark, J. (2013). Does low self-control predict fictitious drug use and untruthfulness? *Deviant Behavior, 34*(3), 242–254.

Musto, D. F. (1973). *The American disease. Origins of narcotic control*. New Haven, CT: Yale University Press.

OAS. (2008). *Results from the 2008 National Survey on drug use and health, national findings*. Rockville, MD: US Department of Health and Human Services http://www.dpft.org/resources/NSDUHresults2008.pdf
Paoli, L., Greenfield, V. A., & Reuter, P. H. (2009). *The world heroin market: Can supply be cut?* Oxford/New York, NY: Oxford University Press.
Paoli, L., Greenfield, V. A., & Zoutendijk, A. (2013). The harms of cocaine trafficking: Applying a new framework for assessment. *Journal of Drug Issues, 43*(4), 407–436.
Parey, M., & Rasul, I. (2015). Measuring the market size for Cannabis: A new approach using forensic economics. http://www.ucl.ac.uk/~uctpimr/research/forensic.pdf.
Pearsons, G., & Hobbs, D. (2001). *Middle market drug distribution*. London: Home Office.
Pudney, S., Badillo, C., Bryan, M., Burton, J., Conti, G., & Iacovou, M. (2006). Estimating the size of the UK illicit drug market. In *Measuring different aspects of problem drug use: Methodological developments*. London: Home Office.
Reid, M. J., Langford, K. H., Grung, M., Gjerde, H., Amundsen, E. J., Morland, J., & Thomas, K. V. (2012). Estimation of cocaine consumption in the community: A critical comparison of the results from three complimentary techniques. *BMJ Open, 2*(6), e001637.
Reuter, P. H. (1996). The mismeasurement of illegal drug markets: The implications of its irrelevance. In S. Pozzo (Ed.), *The underground economy*. Kalamazoo, MI: Upjon Institute for Employment Research.
Reuter, P. H. (2009). Systemic violence in drug markets. *Crime, Law and Social Change, 52*(3), 275–284.
Reuter, P. H. (2014). The mobility of drug trafficking. In LSE (Ed.), *Ending the drug wars. Report of the LSE expert group on the economics of drug policy*. London: The London School of Economics and Political Science.
Reuter, P. H., & Caulkins, J. P. (2004). Illegal "lemons": Price dispersion in cocaine and heroin markets. *Bulletin on Narcotics, 51*(1–2), 141–165.
Reuter, P. H., & Greenfield, V. A. (2001). Measuring global drug markets. How good are the numbers and why should we care about them? *World Economics, 2*(4), 159–173.
Reuter, P. H., & Kleiman, M. A. R. (1986). Risks and prices: An economic analysis of drug enforcement. *Crime and Justice, 7*, 289–340.
Richter, L., & Johnson, P. B. (2001). Current methods of assessing substance use: A review of strengths, problems, and developments. *Journal of Drug Issues, 31*(4), 809–832.
Rossi, C., & Ricci, R. (2009). *Modelling and estimating illicit drug market as a tool to evaluate drug policy: The case of Italy*. Working Paper. http://www.issdp.org/conferences/2009/papers/Rossi_REVISED_Modelling&estimating_illicitdrugmarket.pdf.
Schifano, F., & Corkery, J. (2008). Cocaine/crack cocaine consumption, treatment demand, seizures, related offences, prices, average purity levels and deaths in the UK (1990–2004). *Journal of Psychopharmacology, 22*(1), 71–79.
Škařupová, K. (2014). *The levels of use of opioids, amphetamines and cocaine and associated levels of harm: Summary of scientific evidence*. Lisbon: EMCDDA – European Monitoring Centre for Drugs and Drug Addiction http://www.emcdda.europa.eu/system/files/publications/780/Levels_of_drug_use_and_harm_Literature_review_465346.pdf
Taylor, M., & Potter, G. R. (2013). From "social supply" to "real dealing": Drift, friendship, and trust in drug dealing careers. *Journal of Drug Issues, 43*(4), 392–406.
Trautmann, F., Kilmer, B., & Turnbull, P. (2013). *Further insights into aspects of the illicit EU drugs market*. Luxembourg: Publications Office of the European Union http://ec.europa.eu/justice/anti-drugs/files/eu_market_full.pdf
Turner, C. F., Villarroel, M. A., Rogers, S. M., Eggleston, E., Ganapathi, L., Roman, A. M., & Al-Tayyib, A. (2005). Reducing bias in telephone survey estimates of the prevalence of drug use: A randomized trial of telephone audio-CASI. *Addiction (Abingdon, England), 100*(10), 1432–1444.
UNODC. (2002). *Developing an integrated drug information system, Toolkit*. Vienna: United Nations Office on Drugs and Crime https://www.unodc.org/documents/data-and-analysis/statistics/Drugs/GAP_module_1.pdf

UNODC. (2008). *Primer Estudio Comparativo Sobre Consumo de Drogas y Factores Asociados En Población de 15 a 64 Años*. Lima, Peru: United Nations Office on Drugs and Crime http://www.unodc.org/documents/peru/ElementosOrientadores-Peru-June08.pdf

UNODC. (2010a). *Methodology – World drug report 2010*. UNODC. https://www.unodc.org/documents/data-and-analysis/WDR2010/WDR2010methodology.pdf.

UNODC. (2010b). *World drug report 2010*. Vienna: United Nation Office on Drugs and Crime http://www.unodc.org/documents/wdr/WDR_2010/World_Drug_Report_2010_lo-res.pdf

UNODC. (2011a). *Estimating illicit financial flows resulting from drug trafficking and other transnational organized crimes. Research report*. Vienna: United Nations Office on Drugs and Crime http://www.drugsandalcohol.ie/16151/

UNODC. (2011b). *World drug report – statistical annex: Illicit drug production*. UNODC. http://www.unodc.org/documents/data-and-analysis/WDR2011/StatAnnex-production.pdf.

UNODC. (2014a). *Delta annual reports questionnaire database*. UNODC.

UNODC. (2014b). Individual drug seizures. *Drugs monitoring platform*. https://data.unodc.org/#state:0.

UNODC. (2015a). *Annual report questionnaire. Part four: Extent and patterns of and trends in drug crop cultivation and drug manufacture and trafficking*. United Nations Office on Drugs and Crime. https://www.unodc.org/documents/arq/ARQ_Part_4_English.pdf.

UNODC. (2015b). Drug money and opiate trafficking on the Balkan route. Vienna: UNODC. http://www.unodc.org/unodc/en/frontpage/2015/November/drug-money-and-opiate-trafficking-on-the-balkan-route%2D%2Dfocus-of-new-unodc-report.html?ref=fs1.

UNODC. (2015c). *World drug report 2015*. Vienna: United Nation Office on Drugs and Crime http://www.unodc.org/wdr2015/

UNODC. (2016a). *World drug report 2016*. Vienna: United Nations Office on Drugs and Crime http://www.unodc.org/doc/wdr2016/WORLD_DRUG_REPORT_2016_web.pdf

UNODC. (2016b). *World drug report 2016 – methodology*. Vienna: United Nations Office on Drugs and Crime http://www.unodc.org/doc/wdr2016/WORLD_DRUG_REPORT_2016_web.pdf

UNODC. (2017). *World drug report 2017*. Vienna: United Nations Office on Drugs and Crime https://www.unodc.org/wdr2017/index.html

UNODC. (2018). Individual drug seizures. *UNODC statistics*. https://data.unodc.org/.

Winkler, D., Caulkins, J. P., Behrens, D. A., & Tragler, G. (2004). Estimating the relative efficiency of various forms of prevention at different stages of a drug epidemic. *Socio-Economic Planning Sciences, Special Issue on Dynamic Drug Policy, 38*(1), 43–56.

Conclusion

The use of the expression "illicit financial flow" (IFF) for political and advocacy purposes is gaining momentum. This success is due to the fact that IFF has the ostensible capacity to denote a complex phenomenon: the transnational transfer of money related to illicit activities. The underlying phenomenon itself is serious and warrants close attention because it favors corruption, organized criminal activities, transnational crimes, terrorism, and commercial and tax abuses. Not surprisingly, therefore, international institutions dealing with these serious crimes exploit the term IFF and advocate estimation of the illicit financial flows. In turn, estimates would be useful to determine the scale of the problems, to assess crime reduction and economic development policies, and to concentrate resources and interventions where they are most needed. Yet, it is difficult to calibrate the trade-off between the efficacy of the notion of IFF in the political and advocacy arena and its exploitability for research and policy purposes.

To be as comprehensive and brief as possible, the term risks being generic. The use of IFF as a single label for different activities and practices comes at the cost of losing significant differences, undertones, and details that, on the contrary, would be important in terms of policies and research. For this reason, the current understanding of the IFF phenomenon is poor, and its definition is problematic and much debated. Firstly, "IFF" refers to a plethora of situations substantially different from each other. Secondly, the term is alternatively used to refer to behaviors which are manifestly against the law or to activities which are in contrast with a supposed consensus on the social good.

When it comes to producing indicators of IFFs, these semantic and conceptual issues are mixed with statistical obstacles related to traditional difficulties in measuring crime-related and hidden activities. As a consequence, methods for the estimation of IFFs proposed in the literature have major shortcomings. Most of the available strategies enable neither understanding of the relative importance of the various activities which generate IFFs nor joint consideration of all possible forms of IFF. In a similar manner, the proposed approaches struggle to connect the IFFs

A. Aziani, *Illicit Financial Flows*, SpringerBriefs in Criminology,
https://doi.org/10.1007/978-3-030-01890-0

and their predicate offenses with the methods used to transfer the capital abroad. More in general, several approaches fail to clarify the exact relationship between the underlying concept of IFF and the resulting estimates.

In consideration of these semantic and conceptual obstacles, this book advocates a rethinking of the concept of IFF and its definition. The suggestion is that the term "IFF" should always be associated with a specification of the related illicit activities (e.g., IFFs related to corruption practices, IFFs related to transnational trafficking) and/or the transfer channels exploited (e.g., IFFs related to the smuggling of cash, IFFs related to trade misinvoicing). Then, after reviewing the methods available to estimate the IFFs, the book has proposed the *flow network approach* (FNA), an original strategy for estimation of IFFs directly related to the transnational trafficking of illicit goods – and potential services. While the FNA has several and severe limitations, it advances the understanding of IFFs and their measurement. The FNA has an assessable methodology which yields information on the source of the illicit capital and furnishes estimates that are country-specific and comparable across time.

As by-product, the proposed approach estimates the economic value of trafficking industries. These measurements have a value per se. Estimates of the gross value added generated along the value chain of illicit trafficking can provide insights into the total amount of money potentially available for further IFFs and into the functioning of illicit markets. Nonetheless, our current understanding of illicit markets seems inadequate to develop reliable estimates of IFFs connected to money laundering practices. Researchers have still to develop methods with which to determine what share of illicit proceeds is transferred abroad for laundering purposes and along what paths this capital flows. More generally, a number of issues remain with regard to our understanding of IFFs and even more our capacity to measure them.

How to reveal the connection between the source of illicit capital and methods of transferring it and how to link criminal proceeds to IFFs related to money laundering are unsolved issues; the pathway to an effective conceptualization and operationalization of IFFs is still long. Certainly, also the management of the underlying issues remains a global challenge. Nowadays, there are pressing questions about how the international tax system should be reformed to support the development-fragile economies and about how it should address the challenges posed by the booming digital economy. Important challenges have to be addressed also with respect to the fight against large-scale corruption and organized crime. Loss of capital due to these serious crimes remains a detriment for many countries around the world. Researchers interested in the topic have plenty of opportunities to contribute to the advancement of multiple aspects of the discipline.

Index

A. Aziani, *Illicit Financial Flows*, SpringerBriefs in Criminology,
https://doi.org/10.1007/978-3-030-01890-0

MIX
Papier aus verantwortungsvollen Quellen
Paper from responsible sources
FSC® C105338

If you have any concerns about our products,
you can contact us on
ProductSafety@springernature.com

In case Publisher is established outside the EU,
the EU authorized representative is:
Springer Nature Customer Service Center GmbH
Europaplatz 3, 69115 Heidelberg, Germany

Printed by Libri Plureos GmbH
in Hamburg, Germany